Study Techniques

Linda Ferrill Annis
Ball State University

wcb

Wm. C. Brown Company Publishers
Dubuque, Iowa

Contents

Preface

It is often said that the only certain things in life are death and taxes. However, if you are a student (and almost everyone is at some time in his or her life), it is impossible to escape tests and their accompanying lectures, textbooks, and course papers.

Millions of words and hundreds of books have been written advising students how to deal with these unavoidable features of academic life. Unfortunately, most of this advice has been based on the authors' personal preferences or biases with little, if any, scientific support. Similarly, much of the advice that has been passed down from student to student, from instructor to student, or in study manuals as a kind of folklore has not been scientifically verified. Thus the study techniques that you are presently using may not actually be the most effective methods for you.

This book presents recommendations for effective studying that are based on the results of scientific research. The evidence indicates that the study techniques suggested here are widely applicable and effective. Thus by adopting these study methods, you will be taking the best advantage of what is now known about the scientific basis for studying and you should greatly improve your learning and retention.

Audience

Study Techniques is intended for use in a study skills, reading, or learning skills course that is offered in a Study Skills Center, or in such departments as English, Education, Reading, Developmental Studies, or Learning Skills. The text would also be useful to anyone who would like to read it on his or her own. Readers who adopt the study techniques that are recommended in these pages will improve their learning effectiveness regardless of whether they work through the book on their own or are required to use it for a course.

Organization and Learning Aids

Chapter 1 discusses why study techniques are important, and shows readers how to use the book to become more effective students. Chapter 2 provides the framework for the rest of the book by introducing a three-step theory of verbal learning that involves paying attention, encoding the material in a personally meaningful way, and linking the new material to what is already known. In Chapter 3, these three steps are utilized in suggesting ways to read more effectively. Chapter 4 is devoted to more specific advice for getting the most out of lectures, textbooks, and other media.

Chapter 5 presents some simple-but-effective study techniques such as memory devices and recitation. Chapter 6 is concerned with helping the reader prepare for an exam and then take the exam more efficiently by using a specific four-step plan. Chapter 7 provides help with writing better course papers and essay exams. Chapter 8 summarizes the information that was presented earlier in the book in a concise and action-oriented way. It provides the reader with the specific help that he or she needs to develop a personally effective study plan.

Each chapter begins with objectives that state specifically what the reader should learn from each chapter. In addition, a list of boldfaced Key Terms appears at the beginning of Chapters 1 through 7 to show the important new terms to be introduced. These terms are gathered together in a Glossary at the end of the book where definitions of the terms are provided.

Following the list of terms, each chapter begins with an introductory Overview section, and appropriate chapters conclude with summary sections. Readers are given an immediate opportunity to practice what they have learned and to apply their newly acquired study techniques to their own personal learning materials through a series of Exercises located at the end of each chapter. The index at the end of the book will help the reader locate specific topics quickly. Many illustrations, examples, and summary charts are included throughout to provide additional help in learning the study techniques discussed.

Special Features

This book has evolved from the author's 19 years of teaching experience in both public schools and schools of higher education and the observation that students often are handicapped by an almost complete lack of instruction in "learning how to learn." It is assumed that students know how to study even though they have never received any direct instruction in doing so. Therefore, this book is designed specifically to help students learn how to study.

Study Techniques is concise, readable, and student-oriented. It is specially aimed at helping students do better in school by providing help with their regular assignments and teaching more effective reading skills. In addition, it helps students study for and then take exams by using a recommended four-step plan. Students who have already learned about this organized plan for taking an exam through using a trial version of these materials have commented that just being able to learn about this very effective method for taking tests would be well worth the cost of the entire book!

Another special feature of this book is that it is written in such a way that the individual student can use the book profitably on his or her own as well as in a classroom setting. The book is also unique in using a three-step theory of verbal learning as a framework for tying together the presentation of practical study techniques. Both students and instructors will realize that the study techniques recommended in these pages are experimentally supported and are based not solely on the author's opinions or experiences.

Acknowledgments

I would like to thank my husband David for his support as I wrote this book. He was always available to provide creative ideas and editorial services as my first manuscript reader. His excellent analytical skills and critical thinking abilities have been invaluable to me. It is first to him that this book is dedicated with great appreciation.

I would also like to thank James L. Romig, Senior Editor at Wm. C. Brown, and Susan J. Soley, Associate Developmental Editor, for their great assistance. They have been most helpful all along the way.

I also have had the help of many reviewers at different stages of preparing the book, and their comments have been very beneficial. These reviewers include David M. Andersen of California State University, Northridge, Mary F. Franke of the University of Kentucky, Jan McMannis of Ohio University, John D. Radigan of Syracuse University, James Roth of Spokane Community College, and Susan Schiller of the University of Pittsburgh.

Linda Ferrill Annis

You CAN Be a More Effective Student!   **1**

Objectives

You will learn to manage study time through the use of behavior
modification techniques.

You will learn what to expect in the remainder of the book.

Key Terms

Premack Principle

contingency contract

stimulus control of study
behavior

stimulus

reinforcement

behavior modification

successive approximations

Overview: Effective Study Techniques

This book is called *Study Techniques* because there are, indeed, specific
techniques of studying that you can learn, which will greatly improve your
chances of success in school. If you spend just a few hours reading this
book and working through the exercises, this will help you to become a
better student.

You will learn the three basic steps that are essential for learning from
lectures and reading, and you will learn how to use these three steps in
getting the most out of your lectures and textbooks. You will also become
familiar with some very useful techniques for improving memory, such as
recitation, and how to use the special study techniques called *Key Point
Cards* and the *Paragraph Method.* Knowing how to study for and take tests
is essential for success. You will be provided with practical help in gaining
such "test-wiseness" on both multiple-choice and essay exams. You will
also be given help in another important requirement in some classes—
writing course papers.

Research studies and the experiences of students who have already used these methods provide strong support for the conclusion that these methods also will work for you. This chapter will begin by looking at some practical ways to make the most of your study time.

Why Study Techniques Are Important

The goal of all of your educational instruction is *learning,* which is commonly defined as "a change of behavior." You have learned successfully when you can now do something as simple as printing your name or as difficult as performing a complex mathematical calculation that you could not do before.

The problems occur when people do not learn appropriately, or when they do not learn as efficiently as they or their instructors would like. Instructors are frequently confronted, especially right after they have returned the first test of the course to students, by the students who are concerned about their level of learning.

"But I studied so hard," a student will say. "I studied all week for the test and read all the chapters and went over all my lecture notes and I only got a C—. What really makes me mad is that I *know* Sue barely studied because she lives down the hall from me and yet she got an A. What am I doing wrong and what is Sue doing right?"

That is a really hard question for any instructor to answer. Answering it requires a knowledge of the differences between the two students, such as their prior familiarity with the material, verbal ability, and test-taking ability. It also requires a knowledge of the various study techniques that the two students used.

It has been suggested that differences among students in the amount of learning that occurs are not because good learners possess any one particular quality or utilize a strategy that others do not possess. Instead, these differences occur because good learners are able to call upon a wider range of study techniques.[1] Thus it is quite possible that some of the differences in performance between our two students happen because Sue knows about and is able to use a larger variety of study activities. One of the most important purposes of this book is to equip you with a large variety of effective study techniques that are necessary to improve learning.

Making the Most of Your Study Time

In the following sections, several study techniques will be discussed for making the most effective use of your study time. These techniques include spending enough time studying, changing your own study habits or behavior, and the importance of knowing when to sleep and when to study.

Spending Enough Time

Time is one of your most important learning resources because it is directly under your control. The problem is that frequently it is possible to convince yourself or your instructors that you are spending time studying or listening to a lecture when in reality you are not actually paying attention. An interesting study confirms this tendency of students.[2] Tape recordings were made of class sessions at the University of Chicago. These tapes were then played back, and the students were asked to report the thoughts that they had experienced during the original classroom situation. It was found in 3 lecture classes that only 65% of the reported thoughts were related to the lecture, whereas in 29 discussion classes only 55% of the thoughts that students reported were related to the discussion.

Research makes it quite clear that *there is no substitute for the amount of time spent studying.*[3] An increase in the amount of study time is strongly related to an increase in the amount of learning. In order to learn, you must pay attention, and it is unlikely that you will pay sufficient attention to the material that you are responsible for learning unless you spend enough time studying. Thus you may find it necessary to modify your study behavior in order to increase the amount of time that you devote to learning.

Modifying Your Own Study Behavior

Benjamin Franklin was a creative innovator in many areas. He even devised a method for influencing human behavior that has recently been adapted and proved effective in self-control of study behavior. Franklin believed that carefully applied rewards were more powerful in changing behavior than merely telling people to be good or punishing bad behavior.

Franklin was once approached by a military chaplain who complained that the soldiers were not attending church. He advised the chaplain, "It is, perhaps, below the dignity of your profession to act as steward of the rum, but if you were to deal it out and only just after prayers, you would have them all about you." Franklin tells us that when the chaplain tried this method "never were prayers more generally and more punctually attended; so that I thought this method preferable to the punishment inflicted by some military laws for nonattendance of divine service."[4]

Franklin's recommendations to the chaplain have more recently been restated as the **Premack Principle:**

> Activities which you do not particularly like to engage in (such as studying or cleaning your room) can be encouraged by rewarding them with things that you like (such as watching television or listening to music).[5]

In applying this principle to your own study behavior, you should make performing the activities that you like contingent or dependent upon studying for a designated period of time. Thus you can reward yourself for studying by letting yourself do something you prefer afterwards. For example, you might say to yourself, "*If* I finish reading this chapter tonight, *then* I will call my friend and talk for 15 minutes." This agreement to reward yourself after you have studied is called a **contingency contract.** Note that when you establish a contingency contract like this one with yourself, it is crucial that the reward of calling your friend comes *after,* not *before,* the less preferred task of reading the chapter.

Several studies that use similar but more extensive programs for changing study behavior have found that students' performances in specific university courses improved, their overall grade-point averages improved, and there was an improvement in reading ability.[6] These results are not surprising, given the importance of the amount of time that the students spent studying. Students who use contingency contracts for study behavior are very likely to be spending more hours studying with more learning resulting.

In order to gain self-control over your own behavior, whether it is studying or anything else, it is necessary first to specify exactly what behavior you want to establish or change. Second, it is necessary to become strongly committed to changing this behavior, and, third, to devise techniques that are effective in changing your own behavior. Below is a specific program to gain self-control over your study behavior.[7] These techniques often succeed where plain, old willpower will not.

Specify Behavior to Be Changed
Once you have determined that studying is a problem or that you want to improve your own study habits, the first step in achieving self-control of your study behavior is to establish baseline information about your current study habits. Unless you know how much you are already studying, you will have no basis for judging future improvement. Thus, during the first week of this project, continue studying as you have been, but keep a daily record of your study time. This monitoring in itself may produce desirable behavior changes.

During this first week, also make a list of as many reasons that you can think of for studying and for improving your study behavior. The purpose of this list is to improve the strength of your commitment to studying. Since your rewards for studying will occur later and the rewards for not studying are more immediate (for example, the immediate pleasure of going out on a date versus the more delayed reward of receiving a good grade in a course because you have studied), it is important for you to be committed to improving your study habits.

Bring Behavior Under "Stimulus Control"
Second, you must bring your study behavior under what is called **stimulus control.** In other words, you must establish one (or at most two) places in your environment that are inescapably linked with studying behavior.

This student who is studying in a quiet, well-lighted library free of distracting activities and people, is demonstrating an excellent place for study.

Whenever you are in this location, it should serve as a **stimulus** or signal for you to study. Your response should be that you sit down and study because this behavior is rewarded or positively reinforced. Establishing this **reinforcement** occurs during the third part of the procedure for self-control of study behavior.

The place that you choose as a stimulus for study should be well-lighted, free of distracting activities, noise, and people, and not associated with behavior that is incompatible with studying. An individual study carrel in a library is a good choice because it is usually well-lighted, somewhat isolated from other people and activities, and in a location most compatible with study behavior. You should do all (or most) of your studying in this location and absolutely avoid other incompatible activities such as leisure reading, daydreaming, or snacking.

Goldiamond provides an excellent example of the effectiveness of bringing behavior under stimulus control. The example involves a young woman who had difficulty studying.

The program with the young lady started with human engineering at her desk. Since she felt sleepy when she studied, she was told to replace a 40-W lamp with a good one and to turn her desk away from her bed. It was also decided that her desk was to control study behavior. If she wished to write a letter, she should do so but in the dining room; if she wished to read comic books, she should do so but in the kitchen; if she wished to daydream, she should do so but was to go to another room; at her desk she was to engage in her school work and her school work only.

This girl had previously had a course in behavioral analysis and said, "I know what you're up to. You want that desk to assume stimulus control over me. I'm not going to let any piece of wood run my life for me."

"On the contrary," I said, "you *want* that desk to run you. It is you who decides when to put yourself under the control of your desk. It is like having a sharpened knife in a drawer. You decide when to use it; but when you want one it is ready."

After the first week of the regimen, she came to me and gleefully said, "I spent only 10 minutes at my desk last week."

"Did you study there?" I asked.

"Yes, I did," she said.

"Good," I said, "let's try to double that next week."

For the next few weeks we did not meet, but she subsequently reported that during the last month of the semester she was able to spend three hours a day at her desk for four weeks in a row, something she had been unable to do previously. When she sat at her desk she studied, and when she did other things she left her desk. The variable maintaining this increase in behavior as the semester drew to an end was apparently the forthcoming final examinations.[8]

Establish a Contingency Contract

Once you have established a baseline for study behavior and have brought it under stimulus control, the third step involves establishing personal contingency contracts for study behavior. Based on what your baseline information tells you about your studying behavior, establish a specific goal for yourself that is tied to a particular *action*. For example, you might want to be at your desk studying at 8 A.M. sharp, Monday through Friday, or you might want to spend a minimum of 2 hours a day studying. Whatever your goal, it must be something that you can accomplish with effort, and one that is not impossible. Setting an initial or even final goal of 12 hours of studying a day would probably be very unrealistic. Do not make the goal too difficult at first. If you rarely study for more than 15 minutes at a time and days slip by with no studying at all, then a realistic first goal might be 30 minutes of concentrated studying a day.

After you have determined your specific initial goal, set up a contingency contract with yourself. Tell yourself, "If I do X (whatever your goal is, such as 30 minutes of studying a day), then I will get Y (your reward)."

Contingency Contract for Increasing Amount of Study Time
for (name) _____

    How many hours a day and week do you want to study? Remember
the principle of successive approximations and establish an initial goal
that calls for small and fairly easy approximations of the amount of
studying that might be your ultimate goal. What is your reward going
to be? Fill out the sentence below.

    If I do (a specific action) _____ ,

then I will get (my reward) _____ .

                    Signed _____

                    Date _____

Figure 1.1

Your reward can be anything that you are willing to work for and can take
many forms: a snack, a nap, going to a movie, buying a new article of cloth-
ing, a 5-minute study break, a 30-minute talk with friends. One way to determine what a reward is for you is to think about what you do when you
are free to do whatever you want to do. This activity is a reward for you,
and you can use it to reinforce your less preferred desired goal.

    Your initial contingency contract with yourself should provide immediate
rewards, and should reward rather easily achieved goals. After you achieve
your initial goal, you should increase the goal somewhat. For example,
once you are studying 30 minutes a day, you might increase your goal to
1 hour. When you achieve this particular goal, you again increase your
goal. This process is continued until your ultimate goal is reached. In **behavior modification** terminology, this is called "the principle of **successive approximations.**" Figure 1.1 provides an example of the kind of
contingency contract for increasing study time that you can draw up for
yourself.

    Generally speaking, there is little relationship between the size or cost
of a reward, and its effectiveness. Taking a 10-minute break after reading
a difficult chapter can be more effective in providing an incentive for changing behavior than promising yourself a vacation in Florida when you have
achieved a straight A average for a year because this goal permits frequent, *immediate* rewards for small successes.

    Most of the rewards discussed so far have been tangible and concrete,
but there is also a place for rewarding yourself mentally.[9] You might give
yourself mental pats on the back when you have accomplished even a small
goal. Everyone likes praise, and it can be effective in building self-esteem

even when it comes from yourself. For example, tell yourself mentally how proud you are of finishing the math assignment tonight and reaching your goal.

In developing your contingency contract, be sure to make it positive. Say to yourself, "If I review all my notes for the midterm by Friday, then I will take off Friday night for that movie I have been wanting to see," rather than, "If I do not spend 20 hours studying this week, then I will punish myself by breaking my Saturday night date." The goal is to shape your behavior through positive reinforcement, not punishment. If you do not finish reviewing all of your notes by Friday, as in the example above, then you will miss the reward of the movie but this is not a punishment. According to behavior modification theory, undesired behavior is best left ignored rather than punished. However, if you find yourself missing too many rewards, you may want to review your contracts with yourself to determine if you are asking too much of yourself at once, and to decide whether you need to renegotiate the contract. Remember that your initial contracts should call for small, relatively easy approximations of the ultimately desired behavior.

One persistent problem with self-control of study behavior or any other kind of behavior is that it is possible to "cheat" on your contracts. You may, for example, establish a contract with yourself that if you finish reading three chapters in your history textbook, then you will watch a favorite television show. However, when it comes time for the show, you have only read two chapters, but you convince yourself that you can read the last chapter after the show, so you go ahead and turn on the television. In this situation, it is a toss-up at best whether you will really read the last chapter. It is always essential to use the more preferred activity to ensure the performance of the less perferred activity, but, if no one but you knows about the contract, even the strongest person sometimes falters.

This is why it is often helpful to tell another person about the terms of your personal contingency contract. For example, tell a roommate, spouse, or friend earlier in the evening that you have to finish reading three chapters before you watch the show. Then the person that you told may ask you whether you have finished reading the chapters when he or she sees you watching television, or, at the very least, you will know that the person *may* ask. This often provides the extra incentive that you need to live up to the terms of your contract with yourself (see fig. 1.2).

1. Specify the exact behavior that is to be changed.

2. Bring the behavior under stimulus control.

3. Establish a contingency contract.

Figure 1.2   Summary of three steps toward modifying your study behavior.

When to Sleep and When to Study

Everyone sleeps, and surprisingly enough, the timing of this universal activity appears to have an effect on study activities. Study is affected both by whether the sleeping period comes before or after study, and by what time of night or day the study occurs. Researchers have found that students who slept after memorizing material recalled more than students who stayed awake. Recent studies have confirmed this effect, and that it does not appear to make much difference whether sleep comes immediately after learning or a few hours later.[10] One explanation of this is that sleeping results in less interference with learning than if you stay awake.

Sleeping just before study, however, can have the opposite effect and reduce the amount of learning that takes place. This is called the "prior-sleep effect."[11] However, if you are awakened 2 to 4 hours before learning, the sleep should no longer affect your memory. Some recent research with rats indicates that hormones may be one cause of the prior-sleep effect. During the first 30 minutes, sleep increases the release of a hormone called *somatotrophin*. Levels remain high during the first half of the night and subside during the latter part. When rats were injected with somatotrophin 5 minutes before learning mazes, their memory was severely disrupted, but when they were injected 90 minutes before learning, there was no difference in recall.

If somatotrophin has the same effect on humans, persons who are awakened early in sleep may have poor levels of recall because of high levels of the hormone in their system. However, after being awake for awhile, the hormone level decreases and so does the prior-sleep effect.

The practical advice is clear: It is best to sleep awhile, four hours or more if possible, between the time that you study and the time that you have to remember the material. But do not sleep before you study unless you allow yourself a period of time to thoroughly awaken before you start to study.

Further evidence indicates that late-night study may not be very efficient.[12] The old myth that it is "both noble and efficient to burn the midnight oil to prepare for exams" is certainly doubtful. When night-shift nurses were shown a training film either at 8:30 P.M. or at 4 A.M. and tested later, the group who saw the 4 A.M. film did much worse. Physiological and psychological arousal levels at different times of the 24-hour cycle greatly influence learning proficiency, and the time of day or night at which you learn affects how you remember the content of what you are studying. Thus it may be effective to cram for an exam for tomorrow, but not for next week.

Late-night studying is generally not very efficient or effective.

Learning How to Learn (Using This Book)

In this chapter we have discussed the importance of effective study techniques for increasing learning. The more study techniques you know, the greater your chances for educational success. You have already learned about the importance of the amount of time spent studying, how to draw up a contingency contract for modifying your own study behavior, and the best relationship of sleep and study.

Before presenting additional specific study techniques, we need to discuss the three steps that are essential to verbal learning. After we have identified and analyzed these three steps in Chapter 2, the following chapters will provide you with very practical ways to utilize these steps in learning from textbooks, lectures, and films, and in taking exams and writing course papers. If you use the study techniques that you will find out about in this book, you will greatly enhance your chances for success in school.

Exercises

1. Many of us fool ourselves into thinking that we are spending more concentrated time studying than we really are. Yet research makes it clear that the amount of time that we spend studying is positively related to an increase in the amount of learning. In order to determine *exactly* how much time you actually spend studying, keep a detailed daily record of your total amount of study time for all of your courses for the next week, as well as a separate record for the amount of time that you spend studying for each course. The Time Chart below can be used for keeping your records. In the square for each hour (or draw a line across the middle of the square to represent one-half hour), record your activity for each hour whether it was studying, recreation, eating, sleeping, personal grooming, etc. If you were studying, be sure to specify the exact course for which you were studying.

Time chart

	Sunday	Monday	Tuesday	Wednesday	Thursday	Friday	Saturday
7:00							
8:00							
9:00							
10:00							
11:00							
12:00							
1:00							
2:00							
3:00							
4:00							
5:00							
6:00							
7:00							
8:00							
9:00							
10:00							
11:00							
12:00							

Summary

Total number of hours spent studying _____

List each individual course below and the amount of time spent studying for it:

Course   Total studying time

_____   _____

_____   _____

_____   _____

_____   _____

_____   _____

Recreation total hours   _____

Eating total hours   _____

Sleeping total hours   _____

Personal grooming total hours   _____

Other (specify) total hours   _____

Next spend some time analyzing your results. Were you surprised at your weekly and daily total amount of study time, as well as the amount of time that you spent on each course? Did you study more or less than you expected? Do you see a pattern in the study times that are most effective for you? If you need to increase your total amount of study time or the amount of time that you spent on a specific course, do you see additional times in your schedule that you could use for study?

2. In order to improve your commitment to changing your study behavior, complete the following list.

Reasons for Studying and Improving My Study Behavior

a.

b.

c.

d.

e.

3. It is important to have a specific place in your environment that serves as a stimulus or signal for your study behavior. As discussed earlier, this place should be (1) well-lighted, (2) free of distracting activities, noises, and

should be (1) well-lighted, (2) free of distracting activities, noises, and people, and (3) not associated with behavior that is incompatible with studying. Look over your environment and select the place that will serve as your stimulus for study. Describe it below. Be sure that it meets the three main criteria for an effective study place. As discussed earlier, a quiet study carrel in a library is especially likely to meet these criteria.

4. If you have decided that you would like to modify your own study behavior for a specific course on which you need to spend more time, it is often helpful to draw up your own contingency contract. The following is an example.

Contingency Contract for Study Behavior

for (specific course) ———————— for (name) ————————

1. How many hours a day and week do you want to study for this specific course? Remember the principle of successive approximations and establish an initial goal that calls for small and fairly easy approximations of the amount of studying that might be your ultimate goal. (Think about your current average amount of studying for this course as determined by exercise 1.) What is your reward going to be? Fill out the sentence below.

   If I do (a specific action) _____ ,

   then I will get (my reward) _____ .

2. (optional) In order to provide extra incentive for living up to my personal contingency contract, I will tell (Name) _____ about the terms of my contract.

   Signed _____   Date _____

Notes

1. Michael J. A. Howe and Jean Godfrey, *Student Note Taking as an Aid to Learning* (Exeter, England: Exeter University Teaching Services, 1977).

2. This study by Benjamin Bloom was described by Walter R. Borg in "Time and School Learning," *Newsletter: Beginning Teacher Evaluation Study* (Sacramento: California Commmission for Teacher Preparation and Licensing, March 1979):2-7.

3. Charles W. Fisher et al., *Teaching and Learning in the Elementary Schools: A Summary of the Beginning Teacher Evaluation Study,* Report VII-1 (Sacramento: State Commission for Teacher Preparation and Licensing, September 1978).

4. Benjamin Franklin, "Operational Reinforcement of Prayer" (submitted by B. F. Skinner), *Journal of Applied Behavior Analysis* II (1969):247. Reprinted with permission.

5. David Premack, "Reinforcement Theory," *Nebraska Symposium on Motivation,* Vol. XIII, ed. David Levine (Lincoln: University of Nebraska Press, 1965), pp. 123-188.

6. See, for example, Kristina G. Hayward, Vincent P. Orlando, and Emery P. Bliesmer, "Effectiveness of a Study Management Course for 'Nontraditional' Students," *Reading: Theory, Research, and Practice,* 26th Yearbook of the National Reading Conference, ed. P. David Pearson (Clemson: National Reading Conference, Inc., 1977), pp. 17-20.

7. William M. Beneke and Mary B. Harris, "Teaching Self-Control of Study Behavior," *Behavior Research and Therapy* X (1972):35-41; and Israel Goldiamond, "Self-Control Procedures in Personal Behavior Problems," *Psychological Reports* XVII (1965):851-868, are the sources for several of the suggestions for controlling your own study behavior that are given in this section.

8. Reprinted with permission of author and publisher from: Goldiamond, I. Self-control procedures in personal behavior problems. PSYCHOLOGICAL REPORTS, 1965, 17, 851-868.

9. Edwin C. Bliss, *Getting Things Done: The ABCs of Time Management* (New York: Charles Scribner's Sons, 1976).

10. See Eric Hoddes, "Does Sleep Help You Study?" *Psychology Today,* June 1977, p.69, for a brief review of the research on the effects of sleep and study.

11. This study by Bruce Ekstrand is discussed in Hoddes.

12. See Peter Evans, "Britain in Brief," *APA Monitor,* December 1978, p. 14, for a discussion of a study by Tim Monk and Simon Folkard on the effect of the timing of study and sleep.

Three Steps to Verbal Learning

2

Objectives

You will be introduced to the concept of verbal learning and the three steps that are involved. (This is preparation for the chapters that follow.)

Key Terms

verbal learning

paying attention

principle of least effort

encoding

associative linkages

Overview: Kinds of Learning

As a student, you are presented with abundant opportunities for many kinds of learning. For example, you may be involved in discussions and class activities that can change your feelings or attitudes toward a controversial issue such as abortion or capital punishment. You may also engage in physical activities and perform skills such as jogging or swimming that you were unable to do before.

The main emphasis in most schools, however, is on *verbal* communication, or more specifically, on the information that is to be gained from the written or spoken word. As a student, you are responsible for learning the most important information from lectures, textbooks, and other media. The purpose of this chapter is to describe and then provide you with opportunities to practice the steps that research identifies as being essential to **verbal learning.**

Three Steps to Verbal Learning

According to a well-accepted model of verbal learning, there are three basic kinds of activities that are essential for learning.[1]

The First Step: Paying Attention

The first important step in verbal learning is to notice the material that you are responsible for learning, by **paying attention.** It is common in both written and oral instruction to use special techniques to direct student attention. For example, textbooks often use underlined, italicized, or bold-faced words to direct the reader's attention to important material. During a lecture the speaker may pause or speak louder to emphasize a particular point or may use the blackboard. Questioning students during a lecture is another way of directing student attention. This is especially true when the students do not know who the instructor will call on next.

One problem here is that students may be giving only minimal attention to the instructional material. They appear to be listening to a lecture or they are dutifully turning the pages of a textbook, but, in reality, they are not paying close attention to the critical material. This has been called the **principle of least effort.**[2] If it is possible to short-circuit an instructional task, students may go through the motions of learning without actually paying attention to what the material is supposed to teach them. A common example of this kind of short circuiting would be a student's mechanically underlining the pages of a textbook without thinking about what he or she is underlining. This is why it is so important for instructors to use instructional techniques that require students to direct their attention toward the important material, and for them to use study techniques that will improve their chances of paying attention to the critical material.

The Second Step: The Secret of "Encoding"

Although paying attention is essential for learning to occur, other conditions must be satisfied. Second, you must *encode* the important material. **Encoding** involves putting the material that you heard in a lecture or read in a book or article into a personally meaningful form. This may be done by translating the material into your own words, or by devising a mental picture or representation of what is being said. Figure 2.1 provides examples of the different ways in which six students encoded the important material that they all had heard in the same lecture into their own words. These encoded notes are provided only as examples of how various students translated a lecture into a *personally* meaningful form, and are not necessarily models of ideal encoding.

This was the lecture that all students heard:

The way I've phrased these questions seems to assume, or may give the impression, that the infant at birth, apart from having these specific responses like sucking, vocalizing, crying and so on, that the infant seems to be like some sort of ball of clay, infinitely malleable, and the parents can then mold the baby into whatever type of person they wish. Of course, it isn't like that—not only do the parents have a say in the child's socialization, the infant also has a say. Their own individual characteristics and individual differences will also determine part of the process of socialization. So innate differences among children in terms of their learning ability will affect the socialization process, just as much as differences in the way parents treat their children. If you had the perfect child, it would not be necessary to discipline.

This is how six different students encoded what they heard:

1. Impression that baby is ball of clay—untrue and must be remembered. Innate differences between learning behavior in children and will have as much influence on parental behavior.

2. Even at an early age infants have indiv. characteristics—their development is not entirely dependent upon parents' attitudes and environment.

3. Parents can mold the baby in some ways but the child also determines the process of socialization.

4. Both parents play a part in molding the child's characteristics, though the child plays a part with his own individual characteristics.

5. Seems infant at birth like clay—malleable for parents, not strictly true. Inf. has indiv. characteristics, innate diffs., affect socialization as well as treatments.

6. Infant is malleable and differences between children's learning ability will affect its own socialization, not all up to parents.

Figure 2.1 Examples of personally meaningful encoding.
Source: Adapted from Michael J. A. Howe and Jean Godfrey, Student Note Taking as an Aid to Learning *(Exeter, England: Exeter University Teaching Services, 1977), pp. 79–81. Used with permission.*

The Third Step: Linking the New Material to What You Already Know

The third step is an important one in verbal learning. If the material you have paid attention to, and then encoded in a personally meaningful way, is to last for more than a few seconds and move into your long-term memory so that it will be available for use at a later time, you must develop **associative linkages.** These are relationships between the new meaningfully encoded material and what you already know.

Figure 2.2 An example of how to remember that the Russian word for onion is *look*.

Anderson gives an interesting example of the importance of associative linkages from a series of studies that he conducted, which involved Russian vocabulary tasks.[3] Students were asked to learn pairs like "An onion is a look." Just noticing this pair is unlikely to produce learning. The student has to engage in meaningful processing such as by developing a mental picture of the two letter o's in the Russian word "look" as being two round onions, and then linking the word "look" with two round onions, which brings forth the English word "onions" (see fig. 2.2).

Since people tend to follow the principle of least effort, it is important that students be required by the instructional material itself or by the study techniques that they use to engage in meaningful processing. Of course, meaningful processing is easier in some situations than in others. The author was a participant in one of Anderson's Russian vocabulary studies over 10 years ago. One of the vocabulary pairs that the subjects were required to learn was "A beer is a peevoh." As anyone who has ever had any experience with beer drinkers would agree, it is easy to encode this and associate it with what you already know!

Two Examples: Tying the Three Steps Together

In order to illustrate how to apply the three steps of verbal learning, consider the following examples.

First, let us assume that you are enrolled in an introductory psychology course and are required to learn principles of behavior modification. One of these principles, already discussed briefly in Chapter 1, is the Premack Principle: *Preferred activities can be used to reward less preferred activities.*[4]

You have already decided that this is an important principle to pay attention to and learn because your instructor has told the class that you are responsible for knowing it. As you carefully read over the words of the principle, you should say the information internally to yourself. As you are doing this, try to think of a way in which to encode this material into your own personally meaningful words. For example, you might think to yourself that this principle really means, "Work first, then play," or "You have to do what you would rather not do before you get to do what you would rather do."

Now try to think of a way to associate this principle with what you already know. You might get a mental picture of your grandmother's sitting in her rocking chair and dispensing advice to you as a child when she told you, "Remember, you have to work before you play."

Or you might think of a mother and daughter that you observed recently at a shopping center. The daughter was complaining that she was tired of looking at clothes for her mother and wanted to shop for toys. Her mother said, "All right, if we look for toys now, will you be good later while I shop for clothes?" The daughter nodded enthusiastic agreement. Later, after they have shopped for toys, you see the daughter screaming in anger while the mother shops for clothes. This mother had the Premack Principle *reversed*—play first, then work—and got undesirable results. Associating the Premack Principle with this incorrect example and remembering that it definitely did not work should help you to recall that the correct sequence is *to work first and play later.*

Now let us look at a second, more complex example. Suppose that you are responsible for reading and learning the results of a Gallup Poll that asked a representative sampling of Americans to name the nation's biggest current problem.[5] According to this poll, any election candidate who wishes to strike the political nerve center of the U.S. voting public has to deal head-on with the problems of the high cost of living and inflation as well as the energy problem. Of those surveyed, 63% named inflation as the nation's top problem and 22% chose energy problems. These two problems overshadowed all others including foreign policy (6%), unemployment (6%), dissatisfaction with government (4%), moral decline (3%), and crime and lawlessness (2%). The total comes to more than 100% because some people named more than one problem.

As you carefully read the results of the poll and thus pay close attention to it, you are probably repeating the information to yourself. Now you should try to encode this information in a personally meaningful form by putting it into your own words or by devising a mental picture. You may, for example, translate the percentage figures (for example, 63%) into "63 people out of 100" because this is more meaningful to you than the percentage sign figures themselves. Or you may devise a mental image of a big round pie that represents the major problems listed, then mentally cut out sections of the pie to represent the percentage size of the piece for each problem mentioned with, of course, the biggest piece of the pie marked "high cost of living" (see fig. 2.3).

Next you must link the new material to what you already know. For example, you might think of your last trip to the grocery store and the high cost of groceries. Or you might recall a recent conversation with a retired person who mentioned how difficult it is to live on a fixed income in a time

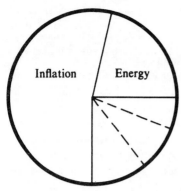

Figure 2.3 An example of how to devise a mental image for the results of the Gallup Poll.

of inflation. Now that you have linked the new material to what you already know, it is more likely that you can provide a correct answer regardless of whether the question is, "What is the nation's biggest problem?" or "What do you know about inflation?"

Summary

Verbal learning results from paying attention to the new material, encoding it in a personally meaningful way, and, finally, associating it with what you already know. This analysis of verbal learning has a clear implication for the use of study techniques: You will learn more when you are required to engage in personally meaningful processing. The following chapters in this book will be concerned with specific study techniques for textbooks and lectures that meet the requirements of the three steps to verbal learning discussed above, and thus maximize the possibility that meaningful processing will occur.

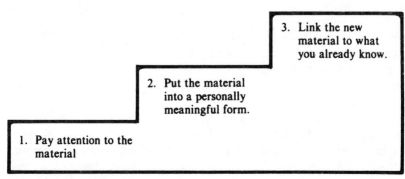

3. Link the new material to what you already know.

2. Put the material into a personally meaningful form.

1. Pay attention to the material

Three steps to verbal learning.

Exercises

1. Think about something that you have learned recently and still remember. Analyze your learning process at the time that you were learning the new material and describe *specifically* what you did to:
   a. *pay attention* to the new material.
   b. *encode* the material into a personally meaningful form.
   c. develop *associative linkages* relating the new material to what you already knew.
2. Look through your class notes for a course that you are now taking and select the notes that you took recently during a one-hour lecture. Read carefully through your notes, paying close attention to the material. Rewrite anything that you do not clearly understand into your own personally meaningful words. Look for ways to relate any new material in your notes to ideas or experiences that you already know. Write notes to yourself in the margins of your class notes about these associative linkages. Repeat this same process with your class notes for other days in this course and for other courses.
3. Select a section from a textbook chapter that you have been assigned to read. Sit down to read the section in a quiet place, with no interruptions, paying close attention to what you are reading. As you read, work at rephrasing the author's words and ideas in ways that are personally meaningful to you. Finally, be on the alert for ideas or information in the section that you can relate in some way to what you already know. Repeat this process as you read other sections in this chapter or your textbooks for other courses.

Notes

1. For a discussion of this model see Richard C. Anderson, "Control of Student Mediating Processes During Verbal Learning and Instruction," *Review of Educational Research* XL (1970):349-369.
2. Benton J. Underwood, "Stimulus Selection in Verbal Learning," *Verbal Behavior and Learning,* eds. Charles N. Cofer and B. S. Musgrave (New York: McGraw-Hill, 1963), pp. 33-48.
3. Anderson, 1970.
4. David Premack, "Reinforcement Theory," *Nebraska Symposium on Motivation,"* Vol. XIII, ed. David Levine (Lincoln: University of Nebraska Press, 1965), pp. 123-188.
5. "Gallup Poll: 60 Percent Name High Cost of Living as Top Problem," *The Muncie Star,* November 18, 1979, Sec. C, p. 13.

Applying the Three Steps of Verbal Learning to Effective Reading

3

Objectives

You will learn how to apply the three steps of verbal learning to effective reading.

Key Terms

surveying

main idea

topic sentence

supporting materials

chunking

Overview: The Three Steps and Reading

Since most schools place an important emphasis on the information that people can gain from written materials such as articles and textbooks, it is important for you to be able to read effectively. To do this, you must be able to locate and understand the most important points in the materials that you are asked to read. The three steps of verbal learning that were discussed in Chapter 2 can be very helpful to you in this task.

This chapter will begin by applying the three steps of verbal learning to effective reading. Next, an article entitled "Glaciers" will be presented, and the three steps will be applied to this example.

Suggestions for Paying Attention to Reading Material

The first step of verbal learning involves paying attention to the material that you are responsible for learning. Therefore, you need to begin by **surveying** the entire article or chapter which you have been assigned to read in order to get a general idea about the important information that is being presented.

There are several different actions that you should take to focus your attention during this initial step of your survey. A list of these activities follows. Remember that your goal during all of these activities is to determine what the most important material is for you to pay attention to during the later encoding and association steps of verbal learning.

1. Determine what *your* purpose is for reading the material. Are you reading it to pass a later essay exam, to provide background for leading a class discussion, or as a reference for a course paper you are writing? Knowing *your* purpose helps you know what to stress during steps two and three.
2. Determine what the author's purpose is. You can often get a clue to the author's purpose by examining the title of the article or chapter, or by skimming the first few sentences. Is the author's goal to provide you with arguments on both sides of an issue, to convert you to his or her opinion, or is it basically a straightforward presentation of information about a topic such as a historical discussion or a review of recent scientific research?
3. Look carefully at the introduction section or the first paragraph or two of the material. Here the author frequently gives you an overview of the important ideas that he or she intends to tell you about in the body of the material.
4. Look over the structure of the material as a whole. How is it organized? What are the main headings and subheadings? Finding these will give you an idea of what topics the author considers to be central and which are less important. Look particularly for headings and key words that are in darker print or italics, as these are likely to be the author's way of telling you what points to stress in your reading. It is especially important to determine the organization of the entire selection because research studies make it clear that we are more likely to remember material when we understand how it is organized.[1]
5. Pay particular attention to illustrations, photographs, tables, graphs, charts, maps. They often contain a lot of concentrated information, and the author has carefully chosen them to reemphasize or provide additional details for important points discussed elsewhere in the text. They frequently serve as arrows to indicate key points that the reader should remember.
6. Finally, note if there is a summary or conclusion section in which the author brings together previously discussed main ideas in a concise way. It is important to pay particular attention to this section as the summary is frequently the place in which the author tells you what he or she considers to be the most important ideas in the material.

How to Encode What You Read

Now that you have surveyed the entire article or chapter, you should proceed immediately to read the material carefully and completely. During the first step, you concentrated on getting an overview of the entire material, but now you are going to concentrate on reading each individual paragraph thoroughly. Your goal will be to determine the most important points in each paragraph. There are two basic study techniques that can help you with

1. Main idea—the general topic of a paragraph that is sometimes directly expressed in a topic sentence

2. Supporting materials—a series of sentences that contain examples, explanations, and various kinds of support for the main idea

Figure 3.1   The two essential elements of a paragraph.

this task, which will be presented in this section. More specific suggestions for taking clear, concise notes on the important ideas that you have found in these paragraphs will be presented in Chapter 4.

How Is the Paragraph Organized?

Your first important task in reading each paragraph is to determine how it is organized. Most well-written paragraphs have two essential elements (see fig. 3.1). The first element is a **main idea,** the general topic of the paragraph. The main idea of a paragraph is what the author is saying about the topic. This is often expressed in a **topic sentence,** which is frequently the first sentence of the paragraph. The topic sentence tells you the main idea of the paragraph.

Some paragraphs, however, do not have a topic sentence that directly tells you the main idea of the paragraph. Instead, the paragraph is composed of sentences containing details, specifics, or examples about the unstated main idea. In order to find the main idea of this kind of paragraph, you have to decide what the one general topic or idea is that is being discussed, which includes within it all of the specific information that was actually given in the paragraph.

The second important element of most paragraphs is a series of sentences providing **supporting materials** for the main idea. In these sentences, the author may provide examples of the main idea, an explanation or clarification of it, or various kinds of support for the main idea. In addition, the paragraph, and particularly those paragraphs at the end of a section, article, or chapter, may end with a summary or conclusion sentence(s). If so, pay particular attention to these because here the entire paragraph is often condensed down to its main concepts.

If the main idea of the paragraph is complex, there may be a series of several paragraphs following it that contain supporting materials. After discussing the second study technique, which is designed to help you with encoding in the next section, there will be a multiple-paragraph example that contains supporting materials.

Asking Yourself Questions

Now that you have determined how a paragraph is organized in terms of main idea, supporting materials, and a possible conclusion, it is time to use the second basic study technique that is designed to help you encode the important information of the paragraph into *your own words.* This study technique involves *making up questions* to ask yourself about the main idea of each paragraph, and then answering your questions in your own words rather than in the author's words. Several research studies have established that students learn much more when they actively construct their own questions about what they are reading rather than merely reading the material.[2] It is best to construct questions about the paragraph that require you to pay close enough attention to provide detailed answers rather than questions that require a simple "Yes" or "No" answer or a factual one-word answer such as a date "1861."

Below is a three-paragraph passage. You are to determine the organization of each paragraph, and then ask and answer your own questions about the main idea of each paragraph. In this example, the second and third paragraphs provide supporting materials for the first paragraph.

Not too many years ago, heart attacks were considered unavoidable. Today, thanks to the work of thousands of medical researchers and doctors, and developments of U.S. industry, many heart attacks are avoidable. Scientists first summarized this information for the American Heart Association in 1964; others have confirmed and expanded it continuously since then.

Research shows that there are four *primary risks* and a number of *contributing factors* that identify a person as having a high risk of heart attack. The *primary risks* are high blood pressure, a high level of blood cholesterol, diabetes, and smoking. The *contributing factors* are advancing age, being male, having a family history of heart disease, being overweight, getting no regular exercise, taking birth control pills, and being unable to handle stress.

Heart attack is a problem of multiple risks. Primary risks and contributing factors act together in ways that multiply their effects. Only your doctor can advise you exactly as to the action appropriate for each individual in your family.[3]

The main idea of the first paragraph is that heart attacks are no longer considered to be unavoidable. This idea is expressed in the first two sentences even though it is not directly stated in one topic sentence. The third sentence supports the main idea of the paragraph by referring to the scientific research that has been done.

Now what kinds of questions can you ask yourself about the main idea of this paragraph and how can you answer them in your own words? You might, for example, ask yourself, "What does the scientific research show about heart attacks?" A sample answer would be, "That heart attacks can be avoided today."

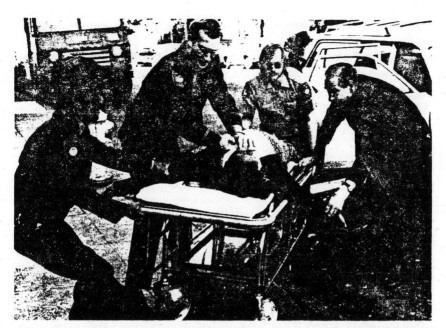

As a result of recent medical developments, heart attacks are no longer considered unavoidable.

The main idea of the second paragraph is that there are various factors associated with heart attacks. More specifically, there are four primary risks and a number of contributing factors. Not only does this paragraph identify factors that are associated with heart attacks, but also it provides further support for the main idea of the first paragraph. Several of the causal factors of heart attacks are within our control and hence many heart attacks can be avoided.

A sample kind of question to ask yourself about the main idea of this paragraph is, "Why are we more able to prevent heart attacks today?" A good answer would be, "Because research has identified four primary risks and several contributing factors that can be avoided to reduce a high risk of heart attack."

The main idea of the third paragraph in the passage is that there is an interaction effect of the primary risks and contributing factors discussed in the second paragraph that multiply the chances of heart attack. Again, there is no one topic sentence for this paragraph. You have to determine for yourself the one general topic or idea that is being discussed that includes within it all the specific information given in the paragraph. The supporting material sentences state that heart attacks are associated with multiple risks, and recommend consulting a doctor for advice on reducing risks.

A good question to ask yourself about the main idea would be, "Why are heart attacks often difficult to prevent?" Your answer should stress the idea that the primary risks and contributing factors interact to multiple risks. Another question to ask would be, "How can the chances of heart attack be reduced?" A good answer would be, "By reducing both primary risks and contributing factors in consultation with a doctor."

The two basic study techniques of determining the organization of a paragraph and then asking and answering your own questions about the important material in it will be useful in helping you encode the material that you have read into a personally meaningful form. Now you are ready to apply the third step of verbal learning to effective reading.

Relating Your Reading to Previous Knowledge

Since research makes it clear that we are most likely to remember material that has been personally encoded and related to what we already know, now is the time for you to develop the kind of associative linkages that we discussed in Chapter 2. Look over the paragraph that you have read and try to remember any previous personal experiences which you might have had that are in any way related to this material. Did the things that you experienced support or not support the author's points? Have you taken any other courses that covered similar material? If so, was the material presented in the same or in a different way? Have you ever read anything else about this topic, and what did the author say? What is your personal opinion about what you read?

Your job during this third step of effective reading is to search for links between all of the things you already know and the new material. The more links you find, the more likely you will be to add the new information to your long-term memory.

For example, a good way to develop associative linkages for the three-paragraph passage on heart attacks would be to remember a neighbor who recently died of a heart attack, and relate what you know about him to the passage. As you think about your neighbor, you realize that he had three of the four primary risks (high blood pressure, high level of blood cholesterol, smoking) and all but one of the contributing factors (advancing age of 60, male, his father died of a heart attack, got no regular exercise, had difficulty handling the stress of his private law practice) identified in the passage as associated with a high risk of heart attack. Even though he had the problem of multiple risks and did not regularly consult a doctor, you realize that his fatal heart attack was not totally unavoidable. As a result of relating your reading of the new passage to what you already know about your neighbor in this personally meaningful way, your chances of remembering the information for later use are much greater.

Summary of the Three-Step Plan for Effective Reading

A three-part plan for effective reading has been described in the preceding section. These are the three important steps to take:

1. Examine the entire passage in order to decide what is important to pay attention to and to learn.
2. Determine the organization of each paragraph in the material, looking for the main idea and supporting materials, then make up questions about the content of each paragraph which you answer in your own words.
3. Link the new material to what you already know.

The last two steps should be repeated with each paragraph in the article or chapter.

Applying the Three Steps to a Longer Passage

The discussion so far has been concerned with effective reading of individual paragraphs and short passages composed of only two or three paragraphs. However, it is important to point out that the three steps to effective paragraph comprehension, as discussed in the previous section, also can be applied to longer chapters, articles, essays, and books. The same basic principles apply except that the sentences of a paragraph become the paragraphs of a longer passage. It is still important to look for the main idea of a longer passage and for the supporting materials.

It also is important to begin reading these longer passages by determining what is essential to pay attention to and to learn. Section headings and subheadings or chapter titles that are printed in italics or boldfaced type can be very helpful here in either directly telling you the main idea of the section or in helping you to identify the main idea of the paragraph in each section. Sometimes there will be one topic paragraph in the section that states the main idea, or there may be a series of paragraphs that contain supporting examples, details, or specifics for the main idea of the section that is not specifically stated.

As you read through a longer passage, stop at the end of each section or subheading and ask yourself questions about the main idea and supporting materials. Then, answer in your own words, just as you stop at the end of each separate paragraph, and ask yourself questions. Finally, it is just as important to link the material in a longer passage to what you already know as it is to link a single paragraph to your previous knowledge.

You can greatly increase your memory for a large body of new information, such as that which is presented in a longer passage, by **chunking** or organizing the new information (ideas, facts, examples, details, concepts) into categories with which you are already familiar.[4] For example, learning the law of gravitation makes it unnecessary to memorize long tables of weights and distances. You can chunk your knowledge about gravitation into a single category by remembering and applying this law:

Every portion of matter attracts every other portion of matter, and the stress between them is proportional to the product of their masses divided by the square of their distance.[5]

The next section of this chapter will demonstrate how to apply the three-step plan for effective reading to an actual article on glaciers.

Applying the Three Steps to an Actual Article

For purposes of the following discussion, let us assume you are enrolled in an introductory geography course and have been assigned to read the article "Glaciers," which is reprinted here. Even though this example involves an article, the same general principles would apply to reading a textbook chapter. An application of the three steps for effective reading follows the article.

Glaciers*

Ice plays a critical role in the water economy of the earth. About 86 per cent of it is in the Antarctic, where it exerts a profound influence on the weather in all parts of the world.

Water is one of the few substances on earth existing in nature in all three physical states—liquid, solid, and gaseous. Altogether our planet contains some 350 million cubic miles of water, most of it, of course, in the oceans. Of the earth's total water budget, not much more than one per cent is in the solid form of ice or snow, and far less than that in the form of water vapor in the atmosphere. Yet these proportions make up a delicate balance which is immensely important to life on the earth. Any appreciable change in the ratios of water, ice and atmospheric moisture would have catastrophic consequences for man and his economy. The ice piled in glaciers on the lands, for instance, exercises a vital control over sea levels, climate and the continents' water supplies.

Glaciers now cover about ten per cent (nearly six million square miles) of the world's land area. Our estimate of the total amount of water in them is only a rough guess, mainly because we have only a hazy notion of the thickness of the Antarctic ice sheet. This vast icecap accounts for about 86 per cent of the world's glacial area. The Greenland icecap makes up another 10 per cent. The remaining 4 per cent is not minor, as far as its effects go, for it includes tens of thousands of square miles of glaciers on mountains in the temperate zones, where they intimately influence man's climate and water supplies.

*From William O. Field, "Glaciers," *Scientific American,* September 1955, pp. 84–92. Copyright © (1955) by Scientific American, Inc. All rights reserved.

Estimates of the total volume of water in the world's glaciers range from about 2.4 million to more than six million cubic miles. If all this ice melted, the level of the world's oceans would rise by something like 65 to 200 feet!

Glaciers can grow only in areas where the snowfall is great enough year after year to exceed the annual rate of melting. Consequently, the ice sheet is not necessarily thickest where the climate is coldest. In Alaska the greatest concentration of glaciers is along the southern coast, which is the warmest part of the Territory but has the heaviest winter snowfall. Parts of northern Greenland are barren of glaciers because there is not enough snowfall.

As snow accumulates, the pressure of the mountainous layers compacts it into ice. Under its own weight ice begins to flow to lower elevations. The rate of flow of glaciers varies tremendously: some move very slowly while others slide as much as 50 feet per day during the summer. At the lower elevations, the glacier melts or discharges icebergs into the sea. But under suitable conditions, the glacier front may advance over the land year after year. It takes only a slight change in the combination of annual snowfall, melting-season temperatures and other meterological conditions to produce an advance or retreat of a glacier.

Probably during most of the earth's history it has been free of glaciers. We are in an exceptional era—neither glacial or nonglacial. During the last million years there have been at least four great ice ages; at their maximum, ice covered about 32 per cent of the world's land surface. The ice ages were separated by long warm intervals during which the glaciers nearly disappeared. At present we seem to be in an in-between stage, somewhere between a glacial and an interglacial age. Some glaciers are growing; others are disappearing.

During the last Ice Age the sea level probably was more than 300 feet lower than now. Over the world the temperatures averaged 7 to 14 degrees colder. There were five continental ice sheets of more than one million square miles each. Three of these, in North America, Europe, and Siberia, have disappeared, but the two in Greenland and Antarctica remain. Mountain glaciers have all shrunk.

Human civilizations began to arise in Western Asia and North Africa just as the European and North American sheets were disappearing. About 3000 B.C. the climate in many, if not all, parts of the world was drier and warmer by two or three degrees than at present. The sea level was apparently five to six feet higher. The glacial region in the Alps was at least 1,000 feet higher than today. Ice in the Artic Ocean probably melted completely each summer. Parts of the temperate regions where small mountain glaciers now furnish the summer water supply must have been arid.

Conditions began to change drastically about 1000 B.C. The climate became colder and more stormy in many parts of the world, and by about 500 B.C. glaciers began to grow again. Then, in the first millennium of the Christian era, came a period of glacier recession. After that glaciers advanced again to a maximum in the 17th to 19th centuries. This resurgence of glaciers was noted directly by observers in the Alps, Scandinavia, and Iceland. Since the latter half of the 19th century, glaciers throughout the world have tended to shrink once again. As a result the sea level has apparently been rising recently at the rate of approximately 2.5 inches per century. Some glaciers, however, have advanced, contrary to the general trend. In parts of the western U.S. there is a growth of glaciers at present which may indicate a changing climate.

Glaciers have been studied seriously for a little more than 100 years. Beginning in 1919 Hans Wison Ahlmann of the University of Stockholm (now Sweden's Ambassador to Norway) introduced a new era in glaciology. He took a new look, in greater detail, at glaciers in Scandinavia, Iceland, Spitsbergen, and northeast Greenland, and his examination led to new methods of measuring their nourishment and wastage. Observations of glaciers are now being made on a systematic basis in several parts of the world. During the last decade, important studies have been carried out in Greenland, especially by Paul Victor's French Polar Expeditions, which determined the volume of the Greenland ice sheet and studied its regimen over a broad area.

The little-known Antarctic ice sheet is more than one and a third times the size of the U.S. and its territories. It covers practically the whole continent of Antartica. Fully three million square miles of the continent have never been seen even from the air. The continent's icecap is known to rise as high as 10,000 feet, but the thickness of the ice has been measured in only a few places.

Table 3.1 Distribution of Water Volume.*

Location	Cubic Miles
Water in the oceans (close estimate)	329,000,000
Water in the atmosphere (rough estimate)	3,600
Water in glaciers (average of high and low estimates)	4,200,000
Water in lakes and rivers (rough estimate)	55,000
Ground water above 12,500 feet (very rough estimate)	1,080,000
Ground water below 12,500 feet (very rough estimate)	19,700,000

Source: William O. Field, "Glaciers," Scientific American, September 1955, p. 90. Reprinted with permission.
*Water budget of the planet earth and its atmosphere is roughly tabulated here. The numbers are in cubic miles. Glaciers account for about 1 percent of the total.

Table 3.2 Distribution of Ice by Area.*

Location	Square Miles
North America	30,890
Canadian Arctic Islands	45,000
Greenland	666,300
South America	9,650
Europe	4,370
Northern Atlantic and European Arctic Islands	45,400
Asia	42,200
Africa	8
Pacific Islands	392
Sub-Antarctica Islands	1,160
Antarctica	5,019,000
World Total	5,864,370

Source: William O. Field, "Glaciers," Scientific American, September 1955, p. 92. Reprinted with permission.
*Areas of the world covered by ice are given in square miles by this table.

Chapter 3

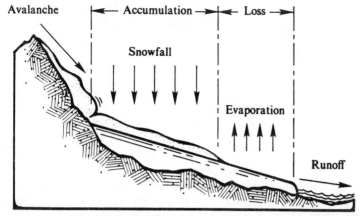

Figure 3.2 The life of a glacier is depicted in this cross section of an ideal valley glacier. Falling snow that is carried by avalanche is compressed into ice, which begins to move by its own weight. The line that divides the areas of accumulation and loss is the *firn line*, where total accumulation equals total melting. Variations in snowfall, temperature, and other conditions determine whether the glacier advances.
Source: William O. Field, "Glaciers," Scientific American, September 1955, p. 86. Reprinted with permission.

A Sample Analysis

My first job is to decide what is important to pay attention to and learn in this article. Since it has been assigned as required reading for my geography class, I think it is safe to assume that I will be tested on its contents at a later time.

Next I need to determine the author's purpose in writing the article. The title itself "Glaciers" makes it pretty clear what the article is about. A look at the first sentence of the first paragraph, which also happens to be a topic sentence, makes it even clearer that the author intends to tell his readers about the importance of glaciers for the entire earth.

Now I need to get an idea of how the whole article is organized. By briefly glancing at the contents of the paragraphs, it appears that the first two paragraphs deal generally with the relationship between water and ice. The next two paragraphs (three and four) seem to give some figures on how many glaciers there are and how much water they contain. Paragraphs five and six provide a description of how glaciers form and grow. Beginning with paragraph seven, the topic appears to shift to a history of the growth and decline of glaciers from the ice ages to the present. The last two paragraphs (eleven and twelve) talk about the study of glaciers and how the huge Antarctic ice sheet is still largely unknown.

The article is followed by some tables (tables 3.1 and 3.2) that provide exact figures for distribution of water volume and distribution of ice by area, which apparently are discussed in less detail in the article itself. The figure on "Life of a Glacier" (fig. 3.2) appears to be something that I will need to come back to and examine carefully because it provides an alternate pictorial explanation of a process that may be harder to understand when it is discussed in words in the article itself.

Unlike many articles, there does not appear to be a summary or conclusion section or paragraph for this material. The last two paragraphs talk about the study of glaciers rather than summarizing the main ideas of the entire article.

Now that I have an idea about the organization of the whole article, I need to carefully read each paragraph. I want to determine the most important ideas in each paragraph by first finding the paragraph's main idea and supporting materials, and then by asking myself questions about the main idea of the material and answering them in my own words.

I begin with the first paragraph. The main idea is certainly the worldwide importance of ice or glaciers, and it is concisely expressed in the first topic sentence. The second sentence just provides a supporting example of the importance of ice specifically in the Antarctic.

It may be hard to make up a question on the main idea of such a short paragraph, but I decide to give it a try. I ask myself, "What is the significance of the world's ice?" I answer my question like this, "Ice plays a very important part in determining the world's weather, and most of the world's supply of ice is in the Antarctic."

Finally, I need to relate what I have read to what I already know. I think back to a childhood trip to Waterton-Glacier International Peace Park in Montana and Canada where I saw my first glacier one *July!* I certainly did not have any idea then that glaciers played such an important part in world weather, but when I remember that glacier I saw, it helps me to remember how important they are to the water economy of the world.

I am now ready for the second paragraph, but I decide it would be more economical to make a little chart for encoding and associating its contents. My chart looks like this:

Main Idea (or Topic Sentence): The proportions of water in liquid, solid, and gaseous form make up a delicate balance that is essential to life on the earth.

Supporting Materials: Most of earth's water is in oceans, less than 1% is solid ice or snow, and even less is water vapor; any change in ratio would upset earth's balance disastrously.

Question/s to Ask Myself: "Why is the earth's ratio of water, ice, and atmospheric vapor so important?"

My Answer (in my own words): The ratio of almost all water and very little solid ice or snow and water vapor work together to maintain the earth's present climate, sea levels, and water supply.

Associative Linkages: That little glacier I saw in Glacier Park may only be part of the less than 1% of the world's water supply that is in solid form, but it has an important influence on world factors like climate.

I decide to use the same chart approach for paragraph three.

Main Idea (or Topic Sentence): Glaciers cover about 10% of the world's land area, but the total amount of water in them can only be estimated since we don't know the thickness of the Antarctic ice sheet.

Supporting Materials: Antarctic ice sheet has 86% of world's glacial area, Greenland icecap has 10%, and other 4% includes glaciers on mountains in temperate zones where they greatly affect climate and water supplies.

Question/s to Ask Myself: How are the glaciers in the world distributed?

My Answer (in my own words): The Antarctic ice sheet has 86%, the Greenland icecap has 10%, and the other 4% are on mountains in the temperate zones.

Associative Linkages: Even though glaciers are rare in our country, they still cover 1 out of every 10 square miles on the total earth.

I continue to use the same chart approach for the fourth paragraph:

Main Idea (or Topic Sentence): There are widely differing estimates of the volume of water in the world's glaciers.

Supporting Materials: Estimates range from 2.4 million to 6 million cubic miles; ocean water levels would rise by 65 to 200 feet if all the glaciers melted.

Question/s to Ask Myself: "What is a possible effect of all the world's glaciers melting?"

My Answer (in my own words): It is estimated the world's sea levels could rise by 65 to 200 feet.

Associative Linkages: It is astounding to realize that all the places on earth less than 65 to 200 feet above sea level could be under water if all the glaciers melted.

After going through the first four paragraphs of the article in this way, I am amazed how much more I know about the important ideas in the material than I usually do when I just read the article. Therefore, I decide to continue working through the rest of the paragraphs in the article using these same techniques. At last I seem to have found some effective study techniques for locating, understanding, and remembering the important points in the material that I read.

Exercises

1. Continue working through the paragraphs of the "Glaciers" article using the techniques described above. For each paragraph in the rest of the article, fill out the following chart:

   Main Idea (or Topic Sentence):

Supporting Materials:

Question/s to Ask Myself:

My Answer (in my own words):

Associative Linkages:

2. The chart used in Exercise 1 for working through the individual paragraphs in the "Glaciers" article can also be adapted for use in summarizing the contents of an entire longer passage. After working through all the individual paragraphs in Exercise 1, according to the directions given above, complete the adapted chart below in order to briefly summarize the complete article on glaciers.

Main Idea/s of Article:

Supporting Materials:

Question/s to Ask Myself:

My Answer (in my own words):

Associative Linkages:

3. Select a relatively short article or chapter that you have been asked to read for one of your courses. Work through the entire material using the techniques described above. First, begin by surveying the complete material to determine the most important information to pay attention to and to learn. Second, work through each individual paragraph to find out how it is organized (main idea and supporting materials); then make up questions about the main idea to ask yourself and answer in your own words through encoding. Third, relate the new material to what you already know. Finally, complete a summary chart for the entire passage like the adapted chart in Exercise 2. Continue to practice these same techniques with the reading material for your other courses.

Notes

1. For example, see Gordon H. Bower, "Organizational Factors in Memory," *Journal of Cognitive Psychology* I (1970): 18-46.

2. See, for example, Lawrence T. Frase and Barry J. Schwartz, "Effect of Question Production and Answering on Prose Recall," *Journal of Educational Psychology* LXVII (1975): 628-635.

3. Adapted from pp. 2-3 of *A Guide to the Good Life,* a booklet produced and distributed for the American Heart Association by Kimberly-Clark Corporation. Reprinted with permission.©American Heart Association.

4. Walter Pauk, *How to Study in College,* 2nd ed. (Boston: Houghton Mifflin, 1974).

5. Pauk, p. 240.

Getting the Most Out of Lectures, Textbooks, and Other Media

4

Objectives

You will learn to take good notes based on an understanding of structural importance.

You will learn how to get the most information out of films and filmstrips.

You will learn how to build a better vocabulary.

Key Terms

note-taking efficiency

structural importance

high-structural importance sentences

low-structural importance sentences

Overview: How This Chapter Can Help You

Lectures and textbooks are both somewhat like the weather. Many people complain about them, but neither instructors nor students do much about changing them. They have been, are, and no doubt will remain very popular ways to transmit information. Your problem is how to learn as much information as possible from the lectures that you attend and the textbooks that you read.

There are only two basic learning activities in which you can engage when you attend a lecture—you can listen only or you can also take notes. However, the choice between even these two kinds of activities immediately raises all kinds of questions. Is it more effective to listen only or to take notes? If you decide to take notes, what are the best kind of notes to take?

There are more activities that you can choose from in reading a textbook. The most common study techniques that college students use are reading only, underlining, and note taking, but students also use various combinations of these and other activities. When you are making a choice among these study techniques, you are also faced with many questions. Which is the most effective study technique that I could use? What are the best kinds of notes to take about a chapter? What kind of information should I include? The research suggests a number of answers that will be of practical benefit to you.

Films and filmstrips are also commonly used in educational situations. Research on the use of these kinds of media indicates that they can very effectively increase learning if the three steps to verbal learning that we previously discussed are applied correctly. This chapter provides you with practical help in doing this. Finally, since a good vocabulary is essential to the most effective use of all study techniques, you will be given helpful suggestions for building your own vocabulary. Thus, as a result of reading this chapter, you will learn practical, effective study techniques for getting the most out of your lectures, textbooks, and other educational experiences.

Research Findings on Lectures and Textbooks

The research that examines the effectiveness of listening versus note taking during a lecture indicates that taking notes is more beneficial. In Crawford's classic study, students were tested by a true-false and essay test immediately after a lecture and again after several days or weeks.[1] Students who took notes generally were superior in all cases.

In the case of textbooks, the research shows that reading the material only is not a very effective study technique. Students may lose interest and not pay attention. Thus they do not actively process the material. You may have experienced this situation yourself: You suddenly find that you are on page 45, and you cannot remember what you have read for the last five pages. You have been turning the pages but that is all!

Underlining as you read can be more effective than simply reading the material. When you underline, you are more active. This increases your attention as well as the probability that you will process the material in a personally meaningful way.

Simply underlining material as you read, however, is not by itself effective. You can fill a page with lines and the result may be little learning and a bunch of lines. Research shows that if you underline the text beyond about four or five lines per page, it will tend to decrease learning.[2] When you underline too much, it becomes a substitute for actually paying attention to and encoding the material. It is like simply turning the pages.

What this shows is that if you use underlining as a study technique, you must be careful not to underline just any point. What you should underline is the most important information. This includes general conclusions, key

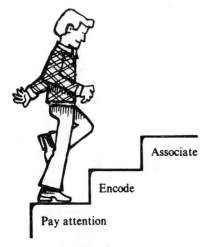

Associate

Encode

Pay attention

Note taking meets the essential requirements for verbal learning.

definitions, and topic sentences as opposed to specific examples that illustrate the key points, minor qualifications, and material in general, which can be ignored without losing the main ideas of the text.

Studies that compare the effectiveness of reading only, underlining, and taking notes on a textbook generally agree that underlining and note taking are more effective than reading only, and note taking is more effective than underlining. For example, in one study students were given a passage to read, and a test consisting of multiple-choice and short-answer questions was used to measure the amount of material that they remembered immediately after reading the passage and five weeks later.[3] In general, note taking was found to be superior to underlining, and both of these techniques were superior to merely reading the text.

Note taking meets the essential requirements for verbal learning. *First,* it requires you to be active. If you are not, you end up with blank pages—not very helpful when you are studying for an exam! Being active improves your chances of paying attention to the text. *Second,* unless you are making a verbatim copy, taking notes requires you to reorganize the passages in a personally meaningful way by putting them into your own words. The material thus becomes *your* material. Note taking requires you to encode the material more than any other study technique. Even when you underline an important sentence, it does not follow that you have translated that sentence in a way that is personally meaningful to you. Thus you may easily forget the point. *Third,* as a result of paying attention and encoding, it is more likely that you will relate the new material to what you already know. This will improve your retention.

The practical advice is fairly clear: It is a good idea to take notes on lectures and reading material. But you need to take *good* notes.

Some Practical Advice on Taking Good Notes

In the sections that follow you will learn some very practical methods for taking good notes. These suggestions include being sure to take correct notes the first time, getting the most important information in your notes, taking efficient notes, and taking advantage of your knowledge of the structure or organization of the material.

Getting It Straight the First Time

In a very interesting study, students were asked to listen to a short passage, and then to write down everything that they could remember from the passage.[4] Then they heard the original passage again. During each of the next three weeks, the students first attempted to write down everything that they could remember about the passage and then they heard it again. The result was: If a student first remembered an idea incorrectly, he or she tended to repeat the mistake during each week even though the student heard the original passage again.

Initial retention is resistant to correction. Hence it is important to get it straight the first time. One way to do this is to read over your lecture notes as soon as possible after a class so that you may correct mistakes and inconsistencies or may check with your instructor or textbook to clarify any misunderstandings. Another suggestion is to compare your notes with a competent classmate's notes right after class and make corrections immediately.

Getting It in Your Notes

If you record a point in your notes, will that help you to remember that information? To answer this question, students were asked to listen to a short passage while they took notes.[5] One week later they were asked to remember as much as they could from the passage. It was found that points appearing in a student's notes were more than *six* times more likely to be remembered than information that was not recorded in the student's notes. If you want to increase your chances of remembering a point, get it down in your notes.

This, of course, does not mean you should write down every point. The result would be a pile of notes that includes, along witih the important ideas, a large number of minor points. These would not be very efficient notes.

Making Your Notes Efficient

One measure of **note-taking efficiency** is to divide the number of important items from the learning material that a person has included in his or her notes by the total number of words in the notes. The more information recorded in the smaller number of words, the higher the note-taking efficiency. Thus if you are recording a great deal of information in a few words, your notes are efficient.

Note-taking efficiency provides some measure of the amount of processing or encoding that has occurred. Since encoding is necessary for verbal learning, one would expect high-efficiency notes to result in greater learning. The research indicates that the higher the note-taking efficiency, the higher the scores on a later test.[6] Thus a good goal for you to work toward in your notes is to record as much as possible of the content of a lecture or textbook in as few words as necessary. This forces you to concentrate on the important information.

Getting the Important Points

Several studies have confirmed the importance of knowing the structure or organization of the material in order to improve learning and retention. For example, students who have been told how a passage is organized, or who can reproduce the organizational structure, or who have been asked to reorganize the material remember more of the information.[7] Despite the existence of many studies that document the importance of knowing the organization of material, other research shows that students are generally unaware of the organizational devices such as introductory paragraphs, topic sentences, section headings, and concluding summaries. These are all aids in identifying what the important points are in the text. Thus to make sure that you have recorded the most important information, you should pay particular attention to these organizational devices. They are like road signs that point you in the right direction.

Johnson has devised an interesting method for determining the structural importance of sentences in a paragraph or article.[8] Different groups of readers were given the same passage to read and were asked to eliminate either one-fourth, one-half, or three-fourths of the sentences in the passage that were least important to the overall meaning of the passage. A count of the average number of times that a sentence *remained* in the passage because it was judged essential to the meaning of the passage provided a measure of its **structural importance.**

High-structural importance sentences are vital to the structure and meaning of the passage and are the more abstract or general statements such as topic sentences, main ideas, or conclusions. In contrast, **low-structural importance sentences** can be eliminated from the passage and yet the main ideas and meaning are still retained. These sentences often provide specific examples, supporting materials, and illustrations of the more general high-structural importance material. Several studies have found that the higher the structural importance of the sentence, the more likely the person will recall the information later.[9] Thus you should take notes on sentences that have high-structural importance (the more general kinds of information) and exclude material of low-structural importance (the more specific information).

Figure 4.1 provides examples of paragraphs taken from the Johnson study. The structural importance ratings of each sentence in the first two paragraphs have already been determined by the method discussed above and are listed below the paragraph. The *higher* the number by the sentence, the greater its structural importance to the meaning of the entire paragraph. The last two paragraphs are provided to give you practice in identifying the sentences with the kinds of information that are most important to the meaning of the paragraph and which should be included in your notes, and the sentences with the kinds of information that are less important and can be omitted. Remember that sentences of high-structural importance contain general information such as topic sentences, the main idea, or conclusions, and sentences of low-structural importance contain more specific information and supporting materials such as examples and

Figure 4.1 Structural importance ratings of sentences in paragraphs.
Source: These paragraphs come from an "Evolution of the Brain" reading passage that has been adapted, in part, from Delas D. Wickens and Donald R. Meyer, Psychology *(New York: Dryden, 1955), pp. 501–9, and also from Norman L. Munn,* Introduction to Psychology *(Boston: Houghton Mifflin, 1946), pp. 42–44. The structural importance ratings come from Ronald E. Johnson as detailed in "Recall of Prose as a Function of the Structural Importance of Linguistic Units,"* Journal of Verbal Learning and Verbal Behavior, *IX (1970), 12–20, and are used with his permission.*

Note: The *higher* the number, the greater the structural importance of the sentence and the more likely its information should be included in your notes.

The study of similarities and differences among the various species clearly demonstrates that whenever there is behavioral resemblance, there is a resemblance of brains. The actual size of the brain is not in itself of great psychological significance, for several animals have brains much larger than man's. The human brain has an average weight of about 3 pounds compared with 10 pounds for an elephant and 14 pounds for a whale. The ratio of brain weight to body weight is much more significant psychologically than mere brain weight. This ratio is about 1/50 for man, 1/500 for the elephant, and 1/10,000 for the whale.

1. The human brain has an average weight of about 3 pounds compared with 10 pounds for an elephant and 14 pounds for a whale.

2. This ratio is about 1/50 for man, 1/500 for the elephant, and 1/10,000 for the whale.

(cont. on next page)

Figure 4.1 (cont.)

3. The actual size of the brain is not in itself of great psychological significance for several animals have brains much larger than man's.

4. The study of similarities and differences among the various species clearly demonstrates that whenever there is behavioral resemblance, there is a resemblance of brains.

5. The ratio of brain weight to body weight is much more significant psychologically than mere brain weight.

> As animals grow larger, more brain tissue must be present for mere sensory and motor connections, and for control of physiological functions such as respiration and digestion. A brain concerned entirely with these elementary tasks, no matter how large, is no more advantageous than a small one which serves the same functions in a small animal. The larger the brain in proportion to body weight, however, the larger the amount of neural tissue not reserved for routine sensory, motor, and physiological activities.

1. A brain concerned entirely with these elementary tasks, no matter how large, is no more advantageous than a small one which serves the same functions in a small animal.

2. The larger the brain in proportion to body weight, however, the larger the amount of neural tissue not reserved for routine sensory, motor, and physiological activities.

3. As animals grow larger, more brain tissue must be present for mere sensory and motor connections, and for control of physiological functions such as respiration and digestion.

Now you try to rate the structural importance of the sentences in the following third and fourth paragraphs. The answers are provided.

> Mammals are distinguished from other animals in that all mammals possess a well-developed cerebral cortex. The cortex is least extensive in the brains of primitive mammals, for such animals have smooth cerebral hemispheres. Beginning with animals like the cat and dog however, a wrinkling becomes apparent. In general, the higher the animal's evolutionary status, the more wrinkled its cerebral cortex. Such wrinkling is due to the fact that the cerebral cortex, which is the covering of the cerebral hemispheres, has evolved faster than the skull case. The area of the cortex thus was able to increase in size only by folding inward (invaginating). In man, the folding is so extensive that more than two thirds of the cerebral cortex is buried in the many fissures that cleave the surface of the hemispheres.
>
> The epileptic is often warned of a coming fit by flashes of light, whirling colors, and similar visual experiences. In such cases, there is frequently irritation of tissues in the visual cortex caused by tumors or other abnormal conditions. This irritation arouses visual experiences such as might occur if the eyes from which the fibers come were themselves stimulated. A patient whose exposed visual cortex was stimulated electrically said she saw "something pink and blue." Stimulated again, but at another point, she saw "a star." Another patient saw "whirling colors" while the surgeon was cutting into his visual cortex.

illustrations. When you have finished ranking the sentences in the paragraphs, check your work using the correct rankings that follow.

Here are the answers to the structural importance ratings of the sentences in the third paragraph in Figure 4.1.

1. Beginning with animals like the cat and the dog, however, a wrinkling becomes apparent.
2. The area of the cortex thus was able to increase in size only by folding inward (invaginating).
3. The cortex is least extensive in the brains of primitive mammals, for such animals have smooth cerebral hemispheres.
4. In man, the folding is so extensive that more than two thirds of the cerebral cortex is buried in the many fissures that cleave the surface of the hemispheres.
5. In general, the higher the animal's evolutionary status, the more wrinkled its cerebral cortex.
6. Such wrinkling is due to the fact that the cerebral cortex, which is the covering of the cerebral hemispheres, has evolved faster than the skull case.
7. Mammals are distinguished from other animals in that all mammals possess a well-developed cerebral cortex.

Here are the answers for the fourth paragraph given above.

Tied for 1. Stimulated again, but at another point, she saw "a star."

Tied for 1. Another patient saw "whirling colors" while the surgeon was cutting into his visual cortex.

3. A patient whose exposed visual cortex was stimulated electrically said she saw "something pink and blue."
4. This irritation arouses visual experiences such as might occur if the eyes from which the fibers come were themselves stimulated.
5. The epileptic is often warned of a coming fit by flashes of light, whirling colors, and similar visual experiences.
6. In such cases there is frequently irritation of tissues in the visual cortex caused by tumors or other abnormal conditions.

The evidence shows that note taking can significantly improve learning and retention. Thus it is a highly recommended study technique. If you wish to remember a point from a lecture or text, you will improve your chances of remembering it if you record it in your notes. But you need to get it correct the first time since you will tend to remember the error even if you are faced with corrections at a later time. If your notes are efficient, that is, they include a great deal of the content of the lecture or textbook in a few words, you also should retain more information. Trying to take efficient notes

1. Get the material down correctly in your notes the first time.

2. Be sure to record any material in your notes that you need to remember.

3. Make efficient notes by recording as much information as possible in as few words as possible.

4. Record sentences of high-structural importance such as topic sentences, main ideas, or conclusions, and omit sentences of low-structural importance such as specific examples, supporting materials, and illustrations.

Figure 4.2   Summary of four practical ways to take good notes.

requires you to focus on the more important information of high-structural importance. If you record this kind of information in your notes, you will improve your learning. Organizational devices such as introductory paragraphs, topic sentences, section headings, and summaries all point to key information (see fig. 4.2).

Watching Films and Filmstrips

Films and filmstrips are commonly used instructional devices in classrooms. They can be used to introduce a topic, to summarize one, or to present additional related material that is not ordinarily covered in the course lectures. In view of the popularity of films and filmstrips, it is somewhat surprising that so little empirical research has been conducted on the effectiveness of these devices. However, there has been enough research carried out to establish a pattern of results with accompanying practical implications for students.

One thing does appear clear from the existing research: Students can learn from films and they usually do learn as much as from a poor instructor.[10] However, the effectiveness of these devices largely depends on the specific way in which they are used.

Generally speaking, students learn more from films and filmstrips if they know in advance what topics, information, or issues to look for, and if these points have been related to the course content. Techniques such as providing students with an outline of main points before the film or filmstrip, providing a written or oral overview of the film or filmstrip before and/or after it is shown, or showing the film twice all were found to increase learning probably because these techniques all direct the student's attention to important aspects of a film.

Only two studies have dealt with the effectiveness of taking notes during the viewing of films or filmstrips. In a study with navy recruits during World

Keep up with the film as it is being shown. Avoid activities that might distract you, such as taking notes.

War II, it was found that the taking of notes during films and filmstrips was of little value.[11] A later study that involved college students revealed that note taking actually interfered with learning from the films.[12] Films lack necessary pauses for note taking. Thus there is a division of attention. The result is that attempting to take notes interferes with learning.

The practical implications of these studies indicate that it is best for you to concentrate your attention on an instructional film when it is being shown, to try to keep up with it, and to avoid any activities such as taking notes that may distract your watching the film as closely as possible. However, devices such as study guides distributed *before* or *after* the film can be helpful in focusing your attention, and you might want to ask your instructors if these handouts can be provided.

These research results are consistent with our previously discussed model of verbal learning. Any study technique that comes before or after a film or filmstrip, and which focuses or intensifies student attention to its most important aspects, such as through outlines or overviews, can be effective in increasing learning. However, a study technique such as note taking, which requires the student to participate by encoding and writing down information right along with a fast-moving film or filmstrip, can actually decrease learning because too many demands at once are made on student attention. Taking notes during films or filmstrips apparently causes too much interference with paying attention—the first important element of verbal learning.

Building Your Vocabulary

All of the study techniques that we discussed previously will be most effective when you have an adequate vocabulary. However, no matter how large your vocabulary is, it is always helpful to know more words. The larger your vocabulary, the easier it will be for you to understand what you read in textbooks for courses and hear in lectures. It will also be easier to use effective study techniques for learning required material and to write better essay exams and course papers when you have a good understanding of what you have read and heard. The purpose of this section is to discuss how you can effectively apply the three steps to verbal learning for building your vocabulary.[13]

The first important step in building your vocabulary requires you to begin to pay attention to the words that you do not know in course lectures, in your reading, and in conversations. Make a mental note of words that you do not understand. You might also want to keep an actual list of "Words to Learn" in your notebook or other convenient place for quick access. It is often helpful to jot a note to yourself about the context or way in which the word was used.

Now that you have identified the words that you want to learn, the second step involves encoding them in a personally meaningful form. The best way to begin this step is by looking up the new word in a dictionary to find its meaning or meanings. It should be noted here that a dictionary is essential for schoolwork and is a required book for many courses. Even if you are not required to buy a dictionary for a specific course, this should be one of your very first educational purchases.

As you read the dictionary definition for the new word that you want to learn, try to think of a personally meaningful way to describe the meaning of the new word. Also note the pronunciation of the word and practice saying it aloud.

Finally, you are ready for the third step of developing associative linkages between the new word, and words, ideas, or experiences with which you are already familiar. You need to find ways to relate the new word to what you already know.

A very convenient way to carry out this three-step plan for increasing your vocabulary involves the use of 3" $\times$ 5" "Vocabulary Cards." On one side of the card carefully print the new word that you want to learn, being certain that you use the correct spelling. If the pronunciation of the word is unusual, write the word again in the way that it is to be pronounced. Also, write a sentence in which the word is used correctly in context. This could be the way that you first noticed the word used in a lecture, in your reading, or in a conversation.

Now turn the card over and write the meaning or definition of the new word *in your own words.* Your ability to do this demonstrates that you have personally encoded the word. The second kind of information on the back of the card should consist of a brief description of how you have associated the new word with what you already know. Relate the new word to any other familiar English or foreign word, to an example, an object, a diagram, a map, or an experience you have had.

Now for a specific example. Let us assume that you are taking a psychology course and have been reading about Piaget's theory of intellectual development. You read in your textbook that the first stage of development is the "sensorimotor" stage.[14] You are not familiar with this word, but you decide that it is important to pay attention to and learn. Thus you prepare the following card:

---

sensorimotor (correct spelling of *new word to learn*)
sen'/so/ri/mo/tor *(pronunciation)*
"During the sensorimotor stage of intellectual development from approximately birth to age 2, infants explore the world through their senses and their muscles."
(original context where new word was noticed in your textbook)

---

developing cognitively through physical exploration of environment (ages 0–2)
(definition in my own words)
the parts of the word itself tell me what it means:
sensori (senses)
motor (muscles)
(associative linkage to what I already know)

After you have prepared several of these "Vocabulary Cards," you can use them as flash cards to drill yourself on the meaning of the new words. Work through the cards first by looking at the word and giving the definition. Now go through the cards a second time and practice looking at the definition first, and then giving the word that was defined. As you work through the cards, divide them into two stacks. Put the cards for the words you have learned in one stack, and put the cards for the words you still need to work on in the other stack.

When you first begin to work on the cards, it is best to go through the cards on your own. But after you feel you have learned the new words, ask a friend to quiz you using the flash cards. It is sometimes easier to convince yourself that you know something than it is to convince someone else. Thus if you can demonstrate to your friend's satisfaction that you know the meanings of the new words, then you can feel confident that you actually have expanded your vocabulary.

Now you need to begin making a conscious effort to *use* these newly learned words appropriately in your everyday writing and conversation. The more you actually use these newly acquired words, the more likely they are to become a part of your permanent vocabulary.

A list of 225 basic vocabulary words that college students need to know is given in Figure 4.3. This is a good list to start with as you begin to expand your vocabulary using the methods described above.

Figure 4.3 List of basic college vocabulary words.
Source: Taken from John Langan, Reading and Study Skills *(New York: McGraw-Hill, 1978), pp. 184–85. Reprinted with permission.*

accede	catharsis	equivocal
accrue	chronic	esoteric
acquisitive	clandestine	expedite
affluence	cliché	exploit
alienation	clique	extraneous
allude	coerce	extricate
ambiguous	cogent	fabricate
ambivalent	complacent	facetious
amenable	condescend (40)	facile
amoral	condone	facilitate
amorphous	congenial	fallacious
anachronism	covert	felicitous
antithetical	culpable	fetid
apathy	cynic	fiasco
appall	debris	flamboyant
arduous	decadent	formidable
assent	demean	fortuitous
astute	deprivation	frivolous (80)
atrophy	derogatory	frugal
austere (20)	deteriorate	gamut
autonomy	diatribe	garrulous
avert	dichotomy	germane
avid	dissipate	glib
banal	dogmatic	goad
belligerent	eclectic	gravity
bizarre	emanate	gullible
bland	empathy	heinous
bourgeois	enhance	heterogeneous
brusque	enigma (60)	homogeneous
callous	enmity	hyperbole
candid	equitable	hypothetical

(cont. on next page)

Figure 4.3 (cont.)

impasse	peremptory	stipulate
impede	perennial	subjugate
imperative	perfunctory (140)	subsequent
impetuous	perimeter	subsidy
implicit	peripheral	substantiate
incredulous	permeate	subterfuge
indiscretion (100)	pernicious	subtle
induce	phobia	succinct
inexorable	physiological	superfluous
ingratiate	poignant	supposition
inhibit	potpourri	surreptitious
innate	precedent	synthesis
innuendo	preclude	tacit
interminable	precocious	tact
inundate	prevalent	tenacious
jurisdiction	procrastinate	tentative
languid	prodigious	terminate
latent	proficient	therapeutic
lethargy	profound	transient (200)
lucid	prognosis	trepidation
lucrative	puberty	truncate
ludicrous	qualm	ubiquitous
magnitude	quintessence (160)	ultimate
malicious	rancor	unique
malignant	rationalize	unwarranted
maneuver	recrimination	usurp
mercenary (120)	redundant	vacillate
meticulous	refute	vacuous
morbid	regression	variable
mundane	relegate	vehement
myriad	reprehensible	verbose
naive	repudiate	vestige
nemesis	repugnant	viable
neurosis	reticent	vicarious
nostalgia	retrospect	vindictive
nuance	revert	virtuosity
nurture	rudimentary	vociferous
obsequious	scrupulous	volatile
ominous	scrutinize	voluble (220)
optimism	sequel	wary
ostensible	skeptic	whimsical
overt	solicit	wry
palatable	sordid (180)	yearn
parochial	specious	zealous

Exercises

1. Select the course in which you are having the most difficulty taking lecture notes. Take notes with particular care for one week in this course. Then ask your course instructor or a competent student in the course to evaluate your notes for the extent to which you have recorded the really important information (material of high-structural importance) and not included minor points (material of low-structural importance).

2. Take your notes from three separate lectures for three different classes. Since research has clearly established that students learn more when they understand the structure of what they are trying to learn, analyze your lecture notes for their organization. See if you can locate the introductory comments, main points, and conclusions in your notes for the three classes.

3. Students learn more when they can record as much information as possible from the lecture or textbook in as few words as possible. To give you practice in note-taking efficiency, take notes on the *article on behavior modification at the end of this chapter*. Then evaluate your notes for the total number of important ideas or points included in them by using the list of 32 Key Points that follows the article. The Key Points are listed in order of their appearance in the behavior modification article, and the list does not necessarily reflect the degree of importance of the Key Points. Also, count the total number of words in your notes. Finally, determine your note-taking efficiency score by using the following formula:

$$\text{Note-Taking Efficiency Score} \quad \frac{\text{Number of Key Points from article recorded in your notes (0-32)}}{\text{Total number of words in your notes}}$$

Remember that the *higher* your score, the higher your note-taking efficiency and hence the more likely that you will be able to remember the important information later.

4. As you listen to a course lecture, jot down five words you are unfamiliar with on a "Words to Learn" list. Also, write down the sentence in which the word was used. Later, after class, prepare a "Vocabulary Card" for each of the words. Use these cards as flash cards to practice learning the meanings of the new words.

5. Jot down 10 words that you do not know the meanings of on a "Words to Learn" list as you read your next textbook assignment. Also, note the sentence in which you encountered the unknown word. After you finish, prepare a "Vocabulary Card" for each of the new words. Add these cards to your set of flash cards for new words to learn.

6. Work through the Basic College Vocabulary List provided in Figure 4.3, marking the words that you do not know. Prepare "Vocabulary Cards" for these words working on groups of 10 cards at a time. Use the cards as flash cards for quizzing yourself on these words in a systematic way until you have added this list of 225 common college words to your everyday working vocabulary.

Behavior Modification* (to accompany Exercise 3 in this chapter.)
Behavior modification means changing behavior by rewarding the kind of behavior you want to encourage and ignoring or disapproving the kind you want to discourage. Used with understanding, it is an effective, caring way to control behavior in school. The case of noisy, disruptive Paul illustrates most behavior modification principles:

> Paul yelled, scuffled, pinched, fidgeted, and drummed his heels all day. He seldom concentrated on anything, much less his schoolwork. Scolding, extra attention, acting disappointed, had short-lived results.
>
> In desperation, his teacher Miss Starr decided to try behavior modification. She first needed to find out how many disturbances Paul made in a day. Ticking them off on a sheet of paper, she counted 23 incidents, which averaged about 1 every 15 minutes. She did this for several days.
>
> Miss Starr knew Paul liked to use the tape recorder more than anything else. "Paul," she said, "Fifteen minutes shouldn't be too long for you to behave. For every 15 minutes that you pay attention to what you are doing and don't disturb other children at work, I'll let you use the tape recorder for 1 minute at the end of the day. You can earn up to 15 minutes of using the tape recorder all by yourself. If you don't earn any time you can't use it at all. I'll set the timer every 15 minutes." She made sure Paul had tasks he could do if he tried and that he understood them. She also checked often to see if he was on the right track, and made sure that he knew his efforts were appreciated.
>
> The next day Paul earned seven minutes with the tape recorder. This meant he'd spent an unprecedented hour and three quarters doing his work! Miss Starr resolutely waited out the other outbursts, saying and doing nothing. Once or twice she sharply reminded him, "Paul, you've just lost another minute!" Her judgments between accceptable and nonacceptable behavior were somewhat lenient at first.
>
> It wasn't long before Paul's disturbances became fewer and less intense. The interval was lengthened first to a half hour, then to an hour. One day Paul said, "I want to use the tape recorder for a project. Do I still need to earn the time?" "*Do* you need to?" asked Miss Starr. Paul grinned and said, "I'll let you know if I do!" Paul remained an excitable child, but his behavior now consistently stayed well within the normal classroom range.

Paul's teacher knew that behavioral scientists believe that all behavior is learned, and that it is learned as a consequence of being associated with a pleasant experience. Paul's behavior was the only way he knew to earn something of value to him, probably simple attention. When and where he had made this unfortunate association of behavior/reward was not important. His behavior didn't cause the problem; it was the problem. Miss Starr didn't try to change his attitude. She worked with an observable piece of behavior that needed to be changed. She didn't try to change Paul's basic personality. She could and did help Paul to control his actions so he and his classmates could settle down to their job of learning.

*Adapted from Clifford K. Madsen and Charles H. Madsen, "You are already using Behavior Modification . . . but until you know *why* and *how,* you might be making mistakes." Reprinted from *Instructor,* October 1971. Copyright © 1971 by The Instructor Publications, Inc. Used by permission.

Miss Starr made use of the learning steps of experience, discrimination, and association. She first structured the situation so he would *experience* good behavior (i.e., gave Paul tasks he could understand and do if he tried, checked often to make sure he was on the right track; let him know his efforts were appreciated). Then she helped him to *discriminate* his behavior by rewarding the desired behavior with tape-recorder time and ignoring undesirable behavior or reminding him sharply he had just lost another minute. Punishment or disapproval was used as little as possible because undesirable consequences can result. Finally, she structured the situation so he would *associate* his desirable behavior with reward (i.e., use tape recorder for one minute.) The task was geared to allow him success, and the reward was paired with signs of approval. Soon he could give up the extrinsic reward and function in the regular classroom reward system.

There are four basic steps of behavior modification:

1. *Pinpoint* Must be very specific and zero in on the exact thing you want student to do and then ensure that this one piece of behavior has a specific, consistently pleasant result; behavior is anything a person does that can be measured, for example, Paul yelled, scuffled, pinched, fidgeted, drummed his heels, and seldom concentrated on anything.

2. *Record* So you know the exact frequency of behavior you are concerned with; for example, Paul had 23 disturbances a day which averaged one every 15 minutes.

3. *Consequate* Set up consequences for behavior; rewards form pleasant associations and promote the behavior being rewarded; to change a child's inappropriate behavior, it is often enough to track down the payoff and eliminate the specific unwanted behavior. It can even be more effective to institute at the same time a reward or system of rewards for desirable behavior to form a new association—M and M's, free time, Green Stamps, money. A reward is anything a person will work for. At first rewards are tangible and then gradually switch to approving behavior that is intrinsically rewarding. For example, Paul earned 1 minute at the tape recorder for every fifteen minutes he paid attention to what he was doing and did not disturb other children at work.

4. *Evaluate* Stay with the program long enough to see whether it will work or not. Remember that ignored behavior will often get worse before it disappears.

There are three more behavioral principles of importance:

1. *Successive approximations* Break task down into approximations of desired terminal behavior, for example, Paul first had to exhibit 15 minutes, then 30 minutes, and then 1 hour of desired behavior to earn time with the tape recorder.

2. *Impossibility of contradictory responses* Interrupting the stimulus–response chain can help break the conditioning. It is impossible to cry if you are laughing, or to stare out the window if you are passing out papers.

3. *Easier to act yourself into a new way of thinking*   than to think your way into a new way of acting; causes and attitudes will be irrelevant when the behavior changes.

Desirable behavior will continue if it continues to be reinforced by naturally occurring events. The goal is to phase out the extrinsic reward gradually so that eventually the person can function effectively in the natural environmental reward system.

32 Key Points for Behavior Modification Article

1. Behavior modification changes behavior by rewarding desirable behavior and ignoring or disapproving undesirable behavior.
2. Effective way to change school behavior.
3. Paul disrupted Miss Starr's class by yelling, fidgeting, etc.
4. Miss Starr counted his disturbances which averaged 1 every 15 minutes or 23 a day.
5. Paul's favorite reward was using the tape recorder.
6. The 15 minutes of paying attention was rewarded with 1 minute of tape-recorder time.
7. Paul was given tasks he could do and teacher encouragement.
8. Outbursts ignored or reminded of lost tape-recorder time.
9. Interval between acceptable behavior and tape behavior reward gradually lengthened to a half hour, then to 1 hour.
10. Eventually Paul gave up extrinsic reward and functioned in regular classroom.
11. Behavior does not cause problem but *is* the problem.
12. Concentrate on learned observable behavior that needs to be changed.
13. Miss Starr structured learning situation so Paul could *experience* good behavior.
14. Next helped him *discriminate* behavior by rewarding desired and ignoring undesirable.
15. Structured situation to *associate* desirable behavior with reward.
16. Finally gave up extrinsic reward and functioned in regular classroom.
17. There are four basic steps of behavior modification.
18. First, *pinpoint* exact behavior wanted from student and pair with specific pleasant results.
19. Behavior = anything measurable.
20. Second, *record* so know exact behavior frequency.
21. Third, establish positive, pleasant *consequences* for behavior.
22. May be sufficient to eliminate payoff for unwanted behavior.
23. Reward = anything person will work for.
24. Gradually switch from tangible to intrinsic rewards.
25. Fourth, *evaluate* progress.
26. Ignored behavior often worsens before disappearing.

27. Successive approximations—break task into gradual approximations of desired behavior.
28. Impossibility of contradictory responses at the same time.
29. Easier to change your behavior than your way of thinking.
30. Causes and attitudes irrelevant when behavior changes.
31. Desirable behavior maintained if continues to be reinforced by naturally occurring events.
32. Goal to gradually end extrinsic reward, and person continues behavior in naturally occurring reward system.

Notes

1. C. C. Crawford, "Some Experimental Studies of the Results of College Note-Taking," *Journal of Educational Research* XII (1925):379-386. There are some studies which do not agree with the general finding that it is best to take notes after a lecture. But these studies generally involved less control over the learners' activities and abilities. See, for example, P. T. McClendon, "An Experimental Study of the Relationship Between the Note-Taking Practices and Listening Comprehension of College Freshmen During Expository Lectures," *Speech Monographs* XXV (1958):222-228.
2. Calvin S. Asay and Edward W. Schneider, "The Effects of Untrained Student-Generated Highlighting on Learning." Unpublished manuscript, 1975.
3. Raymond W. Kulhavy, James W. Dyer, and Linda Silver, "The Effects of Note Taking and Test Expectancy on the Learning of Text Material," *Journal of Educational Research* LXVIII (1975):363-365. There are other studies with conflicting results. But again there are often problems with these studies since they made broad comparisons without taking into account important factors which would influence the results. See, for example, Kalmer E. Stordahl and Clifford M. Christensen, "The Effect of Study Techniques on Comprehension and Retention," *Journal of Educational Research* IL (1956):561-570.
4. Michael J. A. Howe, "Repeated Presentation and Recall of Meaningful Prose," *Journal of Educational Psychology* LVI (1970):214-219.
5. Michael J. A. Howe, "Using Students' Notes to Examine the Role of the Individual Learner in Acquiring Meaningful Subject Matter," *Journal of Educational Research* LXIV (1970):61-63.
6. Ibid.
7. See, for example, Richard K. Staley and Richard I. Wolf, "The Outline as an Encoding and Retrieval Cue in Learning from Prose." Paper presented at the Annual Meetings of the American Educational Research Association, San Francisco, April, 1979; or Raymond W. Kulhavy, Richard F. Schmid, and Carol H. Walker, "Temporal Organization in Prose," *American Educational Research Journal* XIV (1977):115-123.

8. Ronald E. Johnson, "Recall of Prose as a Function of the Structural Importance of Linguistic Units," *Journal of Verbal Learning and Verbal Behavior* IX (1970):12-20.

9. Johnson.

10. For a discussion of the research on films and filmstrips which is only briefly summarized here, see Wilbert J. McKeachie, *Teaching Tips: A Guidebook for the Beginning College Teacher* (Lexington, MA: D. C. Heath, 1969).

11. P. E. Vernon, "An Experiment on the Value of the Film and Film-Strip in the Instruction of Adults," *British Journal of Educational Psychology* XVI (1946):149-162.

12. Philip Ash and Bruce J. Carlton, "The Value of Note-Taking During Film Learning," *British Journal of Educational Psychology* XXIII (1953):121-125.

13. For research studies supporting the use of these recommended study techniques for increasing vocabulary, see Joel R. Levin, Christine B. McCormick, Gloria E. Miller, and Jill K. Berry, "Mnemonic Versus Nonmnemonic Vocabulary-learning Strategies for Children," *American Educational Research Journal* XIX (1982):121-136.

14. J. Piaget, "Piaget's Theory," in *Carmichael's Manual of Child Psychology*, 3rd ed., ed. P. H. Mussen (New York: John Wiley, 1970), pp. 703-732.

Chapter 4

Some Simple-But-Effective Study Techniques 5

Objectives

You will learn a number of techniques for improving your memory.

You will learn how to use recitation or oral summaries to improve your memory and understanding.

You will learn how to write paragraph summaries and use key point cards to learn and remember assigned material.

Key Terms

mnemonics

method of place

peg or hook system

recitation

paragraph method

key point cards

Overview: How This Chapter Can Help You

In this chapter you will learn about some simple and somewhat unusual but very effective special study techniques. These techniques are especially designed to take advantage of the benefits of the three steps to verbal learning. In addition, research has supported the general effectiveness of these study activities.

Mnemonics (Devices for Improving Memory)

If students could remember everything, or even almost everything, that they once read, saw, or heard, their lives and their instructors' would be much simpler. In reality, however, forgetfulness is a problem for students as well as for everyone else. Since the times of the ancient Greeks, people have been searching for ways to improve memory. Over the years a series of

mnemonics (pronounced "newmoniks"), which are methods, devices, or even tricks for improving memory, have been developed.[1] These memory techniques involve the use of mental imagery and mental reorganization in order to provide distinctive cues or signals for later recall.

Until recently there was little or no experimental evidence to support the use of these memory techniques even though users of them gave many enthusiastic testimonials. During the last 10 years, however, there has been a growing body of research evidence that appears to indicate that these mnemonic devices actually come quite close to meeting the demands of our model for effective verbal learning.

Method of Place

Probably the oldest mnemonic device is the **method of place.** This method is said to have been invented around 500 B.C. by a Greek poet named Simonides. The story has been told in the following way:

> Simonides was commissioned to compose a lyric poem praising a Roman nobleman and to recite this panegyric [formal speech in praise of a distinguished person] at a banquet in his honor attended by a multitude of guests. Following his oration before the assembled guests, Simonides was briefly called outside the banqueting hall by a messenger of the gods Castor and Pollux, whom he had also praised in his poem; while he was absent, the roof of the hall collapsed, killing all the celebrants. So mangled were the corpses that relatives were unable to identify them. But Simonides stepped forward and named each of the many corpses on the basis of where they were located in the huge banquet hall. This feat of total recall is said to have convinced Simonides of a basis prescription for remembering—to use an orderly arrangement of locations into which one could place the images of things or people that are to be remembered.[2]

Good memories were very important in ancient times because books, paper, and writing instruments were scarce, and xeroxing, of course, had not been invented. Mnemonic devices were an important part of public speaking, and the speakers frequently used the method of place to help them memorize their speeches.

There are several important steps involved in using this method:[3]

1. The person who is using the method has to choose a well-known street, room, or building where there are as many distinctive locations as there are items in the list to be remembered.
2. Then the person must memorize the list of these locations or "memory snapshots" in a particular order.
3. Next the person must make up a vivid, concrete image for each of the items in the list to be remembered.
4. Then each one of the items in the list to be learned must be mentally associated one by one in some vivid, concrete way with the "mental snapshot" of the distinctive locations in their proper order. The same set of

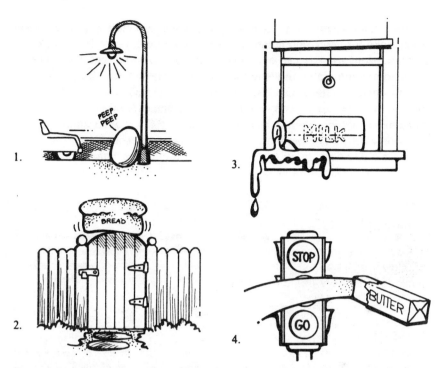

Figure 5.1   The method of place.

loci or distinctive places are used over and over in the same order for learning each new list.

5. Finally the person recalls the list in the appropriate order by mentally "walking" down the street or through the room or building and "reading" off the items as they appear in their distinctive locations.

As an example of applying this method, let us assume that you are trying to remember a grocery list of four items—eggs, bread, milk, and butter. Your distinctive locations, which you have already selected and memorized in the correct order, are on the block in front of your house beginning with a streetlight, your neighbor's arched gate, the windowsill on your house, and the stoplight at the end of the street. Now you must make up a vivid, concrete image for each of the items on the grocery list, and then associate the image with the distinctive location in its proper order. You begin by imagining a large, oval egg leaning against the streetlight, then a rounded loaf of fresh bread precariously balanced on top of the arched gate, the contents of a bottle of milk spilling down from your windowsill, and the yellow butter smeared across the yellow caution light on the stoplight. Now to remember the grocery list all you have to do is to mentally move down your list of memorized distinctive locations beginning with the streetlight and read off the grocery items as you go. (see fig. 5.1).

The strongest anecdotal evidence revealing that this method actually works comes from a fascinating book by A. R. Luria entitled *The Mind of a Mnemonist*.[4] The book makes very interesting reading and is highly recommended because it details the life of a real man who virtually never forgot anything. Luria could remember astoundingly large amounts of information of all kinds and could retain it for many years. Apparently he had discovered the method of place for himself, and relied almost exclusively on vivid mental images and unique personal associations to remember practically everything that had ever happened to him. A quote from Luria's book illustrates this technique:

> When S. read through a long series of words, each word would elicit a graphic image. And since the series was fairly long, he had to find some way of distributing these images of his in a mental row or sequence. Most often (and this habit persisted throughout his life), he would "distribute" them along some roadway or street he visualized in his mind. Sometimes this was a street in his hometown, which would also include the yard attached to the house he had lived in as a child and which he recalled vividly. On the other hand, he might also select a street in Moscow. Frequently he would take a mental walk along that street . . . and slowly make his way down, "distributing" his images at houses, gates, and store windows.
>
> This technique of converting a series of words into a series of graphic images explains why S. could so readily reproduce a series from start to finish in reverse order; how he could rapidly name the word that preceded or followed one I'd select from the series. To do this, he would simply begin his walk, either from the beginning or from the end of the street, find the image of the object I had named, and "take a look at" whatever happened to be situated on either side of it.[5]

On the surface S.'s memory abilities may appear ideal, but, as Luria details in his book, there were associated problems. For instance S. remembered so well that he had difficulty ever forgetting anything. Furthermore, he had difficulty in converting all the particulars he remembered into general concepts, which greatly handicapped him in abstract reasoning.

However, despite these personal difficulties that S. experienced, the method of place appears to be quite effective as is indicated not only by S. and other anecdotal records but also by experimental research. In one study students were asked to learn many lists of words using 40 locations around campus.[6] Lists were presented only once at a rate of about 13 seconds per item. Students were tested immediately when their recall was found to average 38 of the 40 words in their correct order, and 24 hours later when students retained an average of 34 words in their correct order. Even though no control group was used, this performance is quite impressive compared to scores usually earned in such learning experiments. In a similar study that used control students who utilized no mnemonic device, it was found that the mnemonic group retained more than twice as many of the words in their correct order than the controls.[7] Thus the method of place has been proven effective.

One is a

Two is a

Three is a

Four is a

Five is a

Six is

Seven is

Eight is a

Nine is a

Ten is a

Figure 5.2   An illustrated rhyme for learning the peg word system.

Peg or Hook System

Another commonly used mnemonic device is the peg or hook system. In this system items that are to be learned are "hooked" by vivid mental images onto the "pegs" that have already been learned in a certain order.

For lists from 1 to 10 items long, the peg words can be learned very quickly from this rhyme (see fig. 5.2):

> One is a bun, two is a shoe, three is a tree, four is a door, five is a hive, six is sticks, seven is heaven, eight is a gate, nine is a mine, ten is a hen.

Note that all of the peg words are concrete nouns that easily can be vividly associated mentally with the items to be learned. For example, suppose the first word to be learned is "goldfish" and the first peg word is "bun." The student must form a vivid concrete, mental image that associates the goldfish and the bun. A big yellow goldfish with a large red mouth might be imagined biting into a crusty, warm hamburger bun. Recalling the peg word "bun" retrieves the image of the goldfish's chomping on the bun and reminds the student that the first item in the list was goldfish. If the word to be learned is abstract such as "justice," it will be retained better if it is translated into something concrete like the golden scales of justice that can be more easily mentally pictured and associated or hooked onto the peg word.

There is quite a bit of experimental evidence that indicates that the use of the "one is a bun" mnemonic technique is very effective in learning. Students who used this mnemonic technique learned more than control groups not instructed in the use of a peg or hook system regardless of whether they were asked to learn one or many lists.[8]

Rhymes, First Letters, Sentences, or Stories

Another mnemonic technique involves the use of rhymes, first letters, sentences, or stories to provide a meaningful context for remembering items. For example, many people have used the saying, "Richard of York gave Battle in Vain" to recall that the colors of the rainbow are Red, Yellow, Blue, and Violet.

Or, if you are enrolled in a world history course, you might need to remember that Socrates was Plato's teacher who then taught Aristotle. One way to remember the order of these men is to remind yourself that the sequence of Socrates–Plato–Aristotle can be abbreviated into the word SPA by using the first-letters of their names. Then you can remember SPA by imagining all three men sitting around a "spa" in long, white tunics.[9] You could also generate your own meaningful sentences or stories to tie together unrelated items in a list.

There is quite a bit of evidence that the use of rhymes, sentences, and stories to remember new lists of items is very effective, especially for students who produce their own mnemonics. But the evidence for the use of first-letter mnemonics such as "Richard of York gave Battle in Vain" in learning *new* lists is not very supportive.[10] It appears that the effectiveness of first-letter mnemonics lies more in helping students recall the *order* of items that they are already familiar with rather than in their acquisition of *new* lists of items. College students seem to know this as research indicates that they are most likely to use first-word mnemonics when they are asked to recall a long list of words that they are already familiar with in a particular order.[11] It is in precisely these kinds of situations where this technique may be most effective.

Mental Image of Page

A final kind of mnemonic device remains somewhat speculative, but is quite interesting because it deals with an experience that several people have reported. According to these people, they can recall the specific location of some information on a page even though they cannot retrieve the information itself. Or, in other cases, readers may retain a more complete spatial image of a page that serves as a mnemonic device for retrieving some particular item. These students may actually be able to retrieve forgotten items by mentally "reading" their mental image. If the effectiveness of this mnemonic device is experimentally verified, it follows that textbook authors could encourage mental imagery by making greater use of headings and indentations, and that students could increase their use of underlining to improve their mental imagery.

Analyzing and Applying Mnemonics Yourself

The explanation for the effectiveness of mnemonics lies in the last two steps of our model for verbal learning. First, the use of all mnemonic techniques requires that the items to be remembered are organized in a personally meaningful and concrete way. Learning is much faster when using concrete words rather than abstract ones (goldfish vs. justice), and mental images require the use of concrete words. In order to devise an appropriate mental image, the material cannot be only superficially encoded. Second, since the use of mnemonics encourages the development of mental images in which the item to be remembered and the word or location to be associated with it are hooked together in an interacting way, the formation of essential associative linkages (the goldfish's eating the bun) would appear to be greatly facilitated by the use of mnemonic devices.

Some very practical methods for improving memory have been suggested.[12] For example, the best way to learn people's names is by converting them into concrete substitutes. A name like Brown can be easily learned by imagining the person totally covered with a thick coat of brown paint. Even names like Fishter can be converted into concrete substitutes. Break Fishter down into *fish stir* and imagine it as a fish stirring. Then pick out an outstanding feature of Fishter's face and link the image of the name to it. If Fishter has large, deep-set eyes, then the mental image of a fish stirring its eyes with a large spoon might be used to link the mental image with the name Fishter.

The use of mental imagery is also helpful in remembering something likely to be forgotten by linking it with the last thing you are likely to see or do before you need to remember it. One person reported that he never remembered to pick up milk on his way home after work. After he devised a mental image of a big bottle of white milk falling on him from the roof of his car as he opened the car door to drive home from work, he always remembered to arrive home with the milk! Remembering to get the milk thus was "hooked" by the vivid mental image of milk falling from the roof of the car onto the "peg" of getting into the car after work, which was an established part of his routine.

In summary, mnemonic techniques can be very effective especially when you devise your own methods. These devices are effective because they help you to impose as much organization as possible on the material, to make the material as meaningful and concrete as possible through devising mental images, and to ensure that initial encoding is not superficial so that appropriately encoded information will be available when you need to recall it later.

Recitation or Oral Summaries

Francis Bacon was probably the first person to recommend using **recitation** or oral summaries in verbal learning when he wrote in 1620: "If you read anything over 20 times, you will not learn it by heart so easily as if you were to read it only 10, trying to repeat it between whiles, and when memory failed looking at the book."[13]

However, it was not until the early 1900s that the first research investigations into the effectiveness of recitations were conducted. In these studies students were asked to verbally recall as much as they could from material that they had read. These early studies found that recitation was beneficial for all kinds of tasks including the learning of spelling, vocabulary, and even nonsense syllables.[14] A more recent study confirmed the beneficial effect of recitation.[15]

However, there are some studies that have not found such a clear benefit for recitation.[16] These inconsistent results may be explained in terms of the researchers' failure to control for such important factors as student interest and whether prompting or feedback is provided to the students as they recite. Research indicates that the amount of feedback or prompting that is provided to a student is an important factor influencing the effects of recitation. Greater learning occurs when feedback exists.

Besides the research support for the beneficial effects of recitation, it also satisfies the essential conditions for verbal learning. First, you have to pay attention in order to recite. The knowledge that you are going to be required to recite what you have learned may well increase your interest and motivation to learn.

Second, the very act of recitation requires that you actively process and reorganize the learning material and then encode it in a personally meaningful way, or you literally will have nothing to say when you are asked to recite.

Third, you will have difficulty in reciting what you have learned unless you have performed the active associational and coding processes that are necessary to meaningfully link what you already know to the new material. If, for example, you are going to have to recite that *aqua* is the Latin word for water, you will no doubt be more successful if you can come up

Recitation is a very effective study technique, particularly if the audience who is listening to it provides feedback by adding what was left out and correcting errors.

with something like a mental image of a beautiful aqua-colored body of water you once saw in order to associatively link the two words. The act of recitation thus encourages the formation of the associative linkages that are so important to verbal learning.

Recitation is thus a recommended study technique. Remember that if you use this method, you should arrange for someone to listen to you in order to add what you leave out and correct your errors. The beneficial effects of recitation will increase if you get feedback and prompting.

The Paragraph Method

An instructor does not have to be in the classroom long before his or her students ask for advice on how to study. This author is no exception, and for many years has recommended the use of the **paragraph method.**

In using the paragraph method, you should carefully follow these steps:

1. First, sit down in a quiet room at your desk with your feet on the floor, have an open textbook turned to the first page of the chapter that you are assigned to read propped before you, and have clean pages of notebook paper and sharpened pencils ready.
2. Then, copy the title of the chapter and any initial chapter subheading if there is one.
3. Next, read the first paragraph of the chapter and stop reading.

Below are sample paragraph summaries for the "Analyzing and Applying Mnemonics" section of this chapter. Since there are four paragraphs in this section, there should be four brief summaries of the paragraphs. These summaries are only *examples*. What is most important is that the summaries should make sense to the person who writes them and should provide a meaningful condensation and encoding of the most important points in the paragraphs.

Paragraph 1. Effectiveness of mnemonics lies in requiring meaningful and concrete encoding; it also encourages associatively linking or hooking new material to memorized pegs.

Paragraph 2. Convert names to concrete substitutes (e.g., Mr. Green to his green shirt).

Paragraph 3. Improve memory by using mental imagery to hook something you will remember onto something you will likely forget (e.g., milk falling from car).

Paragraph 4. Mnemonic devices improve memory by helping determine meaning and structure of material; encode material in a meaningful and concrete way so that good retrieval cues are available later.

Figure 5.3   Examples of using the paragraph method.

4. Then, carefully think over what you have just read and, in *as few words as possible* and *in your own words*, write a brief summary of what you read. The summary may be only four or five words long and need not be written in sentence form. Figure 5.3 provides examples of brief paragraph summaries written for the section on "Analyzing and Applying Mnemonics" earlier in this chapter.

5. Continue reading the chapter in this manner, stopping to summarize in your own words after you read each paragraph. Copy the chapter subheadings into your notes between the appropriate paragraphs.

6. It is important that you not write too much or you will end up transcribing the whole work. A good guideline is that it should be possible to summarize most college textbook chapters on both sides of three pages of regular notebook size ($8\frac{1}{2}'' \times 11''$) paper.

7. The real benefits of this system become apparent when it is time to study for an exam. If you have done the chapter summaries well, it will be possible for you to review from a series of three-page summaries rather than having to read or reread the entire textbook assignment.

This kind of system has been recommended to hundreds of students over many years, and the feedback from these students has generally been quite favorable. Even though there was no research evidence for the effectiveness of this technique until recently, these beneficial results might well be expected when the paragraph method is analyzed in terms of meeting the demands of our model of verbal learning.

Step 1 increases the chances that you will pay attention because if you do not direct your attention to the learning material, you will not have any paragraph summaries written down. Steps 2 through 6 require you to closely examine the words and sentences in the paragraph in order to find personally meaningful retrieval cues. These personally encoded cues are then associatively linked to what you already know or have experienced. Thus you construct your own meaning for the paragraph, which is reflected in your paragraph summary that you wrote in your own words. Steps 2 and 5 help you to analyze the organization of the entire passage by writing down chapter subheadings, and there is general research agreement that one of the best ways to remember information from material is to figure out how it is organized. Step 4's emphasis on summarizing the paragraph in as few words as possible is supported by research that found that note-taking efficiency (a maximum amount of information recorded in a minimum number of words) was positively related to higher meaningful recall. Step 7 stresses the importance of reviewing before exams, which is almost universally accepted as important.

A recent study tested the effects of requiring students to actively construct meaning for text material through the use of these kinds of paragraph summaries.[17] The results indicated that these summaries increased learning.

Using Key Point Cards

The use of **key point cards** is related to the paragraph method, and may be used as an alternative study technique. Even though there is no specific research support for this method, it has been recommended frequently to students, and the resulting feedback has been very positive.

The key point card method works best with a textbook in which the author has provided the reader with some idea of what the author considers to be the most important material in the chapters. This may be done through an outline at the beginning of each chapter or through a summary of important ideas at the end of each chapter. If the author has not provided an indication of the most important material, then it is up to the reader to determine the key points or the most important information based on such areas as what the author emphasizes in the paragraphs, what the instructor stresses in class, or what is listed in a course syllabus. Key point cards can also be made for the most important points in lectures.

Once you determine the key points, then you will need a set of 3" X 5" file cards. On one side, write the key point itself and give the page number on which it is discussed in the textbook or the date of the lecture notes in which it was discussed. Then on the other side of the card, write a brief definition *in your own words* of the meaning of the key point.

For example, let us assume you are taking a course in human growth and development and are required to learn the three stages of prenatal development (germinal, embryonic, fetal). Since the importance of these terms has been stressed again and again in course lectures and in the textbook, you decide to make key point cards for these three stages. Sample cards are shown in Figure 5.4. Remember there is no perfect way to make a key point card. What is most important is that you encode the material in a brief and personally meaningful way.

It is a good idea to keep all of the key point cards for a chapter or lecture section bound together with a rubber band, and continue making a set of cards for each chapter or lecture section. The benefits of this method become obvious when you begin to review for an exam since you have organized together in one place and in a personally meaningful way the main ideas that you are responsible for learning. It is also possible to use the key point cards as a set of flash cards for review. You can go through the key point cards by either looking at the definitions and identifying the main points, or by looking at the key points and providing the definitions. You can also ask another person to use the cards to quiz you on your knowledge of the material.

Front of card   Back of card

germinal stage p. 10 of text 11/10 lecture notes	period from conception to end of second week after conception; technically ends when fertilized ovum embeds in uterine wall
embryo p. 12 of text 11/10 lecture notes	period of 6 weeks from end of 2nd week until end of 2nd month, tech. ends when first bone cell laid down; at end of stage 95% of body parts laid down and looks like miniature human being
fetus p. 15 of text 11/10 lecture notes	lasts 7 months from end of 2nd month to birth; further growth and dev. of body structures laid down during embryonic stage

Figure 5.4   Sample key point cards.

The reported success of this study technique would seem to be explained in much the same way as the paragraph method in terms of our model of verbal learning. First, the physical preparation of the key point cards requires you to pay attention to the material. Identifying the key points of the material to be learned helps you figure out how the material is organized, and knowing how the material is organized has been associated with increased learning. Finally, writing the definitions of the key points on the reverse side of the cards helps you to encode the material in a personally meaningful way and then associate it with what you already know. Using the key point cards as flash cards before an exam helps you to focus your efforts during the very important process of reviewing.

Exercises

1. Mnemonic devices can be very useful for remembering information because they help you elaborate and visualize the material to be learned in a meaningful way and then help you associate items. Practice these techniques by devising some mnemonics for remembering the following information:

   a. Use the method of place to remember the following list of groceries that you want to buy: laundry detergent, tomatoes, string, milk, bread, and cookies.

   b. Use the peg or hook system to remember the taxonomy or classification of plants and animals you may have learned in biology: Kingdom, Phylum, Class, Order, Family, Genus, Species, Variety. Remember if the word you are trying to learn is abstract like *Phylum,* you will remember it better if you first translate it into a concrete noun like a file, for example, which sounds the same.

c. Imagine you are at a party and have met people with the following names. Devise a mnemonic device to help you remember each person's name. You might use a concrete substitute for a name (the more vivid the mental image, the better you will recall the name), you might associate the name with someone or something you already know, or you might make up a simple rhyme for the person's name.

   (1) Jane Johnson
   (2) Ron Hanson
   (3) Richard Green
   (4) Bonnie Smith
   (5) Benji Abbott
   (6) Karen Carpenter

d. Imagine that you are in a geography class and have been asked to learn the names of the Great Lakes (Michigan, Ontario, Erie, Huron, and Superior). Make up four different mnemonic devices using rhymes, first letters, a sentence, and a story to help you remember the names of the five Great Lakes.

2. Oral recitations can be a very effective study technique. Since you may not have used this study technique before, it can be helpful to practice recitation. Reread the section on "Recitation or Oral Summaries." Find a friend or another student who will also be willing to read this section of the chapter and then listen to you recite what you have learned about recitation. In your recitation to your friend be sure to include:

   a. a brief review of the research on recitation.
   b. possible explanations for the effectiveness of recitation based on our three-part model of verbal learning.
   c. a brief summary of the best ways for students to use recitation.

   Remember that it is important for the person who is listening to your recitation to add anything you may have left out and to correct your mistakes. Continue to practice recitation in this way using materials from your other courses.

3. Use of the paragraph method for taking notes has been associated with increased learning. Practice using the paragraph method for notes on the section on "Watching Films and Filmstrips" in Chapter 4. Remember that you are to briefly summarize the contents of each paragraph *in your own words*. Since the section on "Films and Filmstrips" is made up of six paragraphs, you should write a brief summary of each paragraph for your notes. When you have finished your paragraph summaries, turn to an example of using the paragraph method in the section that follows these exercises. This example is not the only way or even the best way to take notes on the material, but it does serve as a specific example of how to use the paragraph method. Compare your summaries to these sample paragraph method summaries, but remember that the most important thing is for your summaries to be *personally meaningful* to you. Continue to practice using the paragraph method on other sections of this book and with your textbooks for other courses.

4. In the section on mnemonic devices, four specific kinds of devices were discussed: Method of Place, Peg or Hook System, Rhymes, First Letters,

Sentences, or Stories, and Mental Image of Page. Prepare a Key Point Card for each of these four devices according to the instructions in this chapter. Write the specific device on one side of a card, and on the other side write a brief description of this kind of mnemonic device in your own words.

Go ahead to practice the making of Key Point Cards with other sections in this book and with your textbooks for other courses.

Sample Paragraph Method Summaries for Exercise 3 about the "Watching Films and Filmstrips" Section in chapter 4

Paragraph 1
Films and filmstrips commonly used in schools but little empirical research on effectiveness

Paragraph 2
Clear that students can learn from films if used effectively

Paragraph 3
Students learn more if know in advance what important points to look for and if related to course content

Paragraph 4
Note taking *can* interfere with learning from films if interferes with paying attention

Paragraph 5
Students learn best if concentrate on film while shown, and have study guide before or after film to focus attention

Paragraph 6
Taking notes *during* film can interfere too much with important job of paying attention

Notes

1. For more detailed instructions on the use of the mnemonic techniques that are only initially introduced in this section, see Harry Lorayne, *How to Develop a Super-Power Memory* (New York: Thomas & Preston, 1958); and Harry Lorayne and Jerry Lucas, *The Memory Book* (New York: Stein and Day, 1974); or Francis A. Yates, *The Art of Memory* (Chicago: University of Chicago Press, 1966). (Jerry Lucas is the basketball star who is a Phi Beta Kappa graduate of Ohio State University.)

2. Gordon H. Bower, "Analysis of a Mnemonic Device," *American Scientist* LVIII (1970): 496.

3. Gordon H. Bower and Peter Morris, "Practical Suggestions for Human Learning and Remembering," *Adult Learning: Psychological Research and Applications,* ed. Michael J. A. Howe (New York: John Wiley, 1977), pp. 125–144.

4. Alexander R. Luria, *The Mind of a Mnemonist* (New York: Basic Books, 1968).

5. Luria, pp. 31–33.

6. John Ross and Kerry Ann Lawrence, "Some Observations on Memory Artifice," *Psychonomic Science* XIII (1968): 107-108.

7. L. D. Groninger, "Mnemonic Imagery and Forgetting," *Psychonomic Science* XXIII (1971): 161.

8. See, for example, P. E. Morris and R. Reid, "The Repeated Use of Mnemonic Imagery," *Psychonomic Science* XX (1970): 337.

9. This example was suggested by Robert F. Biehler, *Study Guide for Child Development: An Introduction* (Boston: Houghton Mifflin, 1976), p. x.

10. Morris and Reid.

11. K. A. Blick, J. Bounassissi, and C. E. Boltwood, "Mnemonic Techniques Used by College Students in Serial Learning," *Psychological Reports* XXXI (1972): 983.

12. Lorayne, *How to Develop a Super-Power Memory.*

13. Francis Bacon, *Novum Organum,* ed. J. Devey (New York: Collier 1902), p. 229. (Originally published 1620.)

14. See, for example, Arthur I. Gates, "Recitation as a Factor in Memorizing," *Archives of Psychology* XXVI (1917): 1-104; or George Forlano, *School Learning with Various Methods of Practice and Rewards,* a report prepared by Bureau of Publications, Teachers College (New York: Columbia University Press, 1936).

15. Stephen M. Ross and Francis J. DiVesta, "Oral Summary as a Review Strategy for Enhancing Recall of Textual Material," *Journal of Educational Psychology* LXVIII (1976): 689-695.

16. See, for example, a review of the literature by Paul D. Weener, "Note Taking and Student Verbalization as Instrumental Learning Activities," *Instructional Science* XXXVII (1974): 51-74.

17. Marleen Doctorow, M. C. Wittrock, and Carolyn Marks, "Generative Processes in Learning Comprehension," *Journal of Educational Psychology* LXX (1978): 109-118.

Test-Wiseness and How to Get It

6

Objectives

You will learn how to prepare for and take tests in ways that will maximize your performance.

You will learn about the effect of cramming for standardized tests.

Key Terms

test-wiseness

reviewing

cramming

spaced reviews

massed reviews

Overview: Developing Test-Wiseness

Tests traditionally strike fear in students' hearts. Even though it may never be possible for you to actually welcome tests, many empirically supported suggestions are now available to help you develop **test-wiseness** so that you can improve your test preparation and test performance at the same time that you reduce your test anxiety.

Preparing for Examinations

You will be in a much better position for undertaking final preparations for an exam if you have followed the suggestions given earlier in this text. If you have been following a self-behavior modification program, for example, it is likely that you will have already read all the material that is to be covered on the exam. If you have underlined or taken notes on the reading material, or, even better, used the paragraph method or the key point card method to boil down the important parts of six weeks or a term's worth of

This kind of testing situation is a common experience in students' lives.

material to more manageable proportions, then you probably have paid attention to, encoded, and formed meaningful associations for the assigned material. If you have faithfully attended class lectures and discussions and taken a complete set of lecture notes, then the effort involved in writing down in your own words what you heard has no doubt encouraged meaningful encoding of the material.

Assuming that you have been "keeping up" with the class reasonably well all along, there are several activities, supported by research evidence, that appear to be very helpful during the last few days of preparation before an exam. These activities involve reviewing rather than cramming, "taking notes on the notes" previously taken in the paragraph method, and finding out the exact kind of test to expect (see fig. 6.1).

Reviewing, Not Cramming

It may well be that reviewing has an undeserved bad reputation among students. Students will sometimes even say that by the time an exam comes around they either know the material or they do not, and nothing they can

1. Review the material over a period of time rather than depending on last-minute cramming.

2. Take further condensed notes on your previously prepared notes to help you mentally reorganize, encode, and review the material.

3. Find out the kind of test you are taking so you can study more appropriately.

Figure 6.1 How to prepare for an exam.

do at this late date will help. Carrying this reasoning one step further, one student even said that the best way to prepare for an exam the night before was to go to a movie! However, this is definitely an unsupported recommendation and could get even the best student in difficulty. Perhaps the key to this student's fatalism about preparing for tests lies in confusion of the terms *reviewing* and *cramming.*

Reviewing involves any effort to "go over," brush up on, or organize *previously learned* material. Review can occur anytime from immediately after the original learning to immediately before an exam. The studies on note taking are unanimous in finding that students who are allowed to review their notes before an exam recall more material. In fact, if there is one thing that is clear from the existing literature on study techniques as well as on learning in general, it is: *Review of previously learned material leads to increased learning and decreases the amount of forgetting.*

Cramming, however, is a different story. Cramming involves attempting to master a great deal of *new* material immediately before an exam. It is a last-minute, last-ditch attempt to avoid disaster on an exam. The widely different effects of reviewing and cramming can be explained at least partially by a discussion of the processes of human forgetting.

Early research with learning established a Curve of Forgetting (fig. 6.2).[1] Although meaningful material is retained better than nonsense material, the same principles of forgetting apply. Ebbinghaus, working with nonsense syllables, found that 42% of forgetting took place after 20 minutes, 56% after 60 minutes, 64% after 9 hours, 66% after 24 hours, 75% after 6 days, and 79% after 31 days. A great deal of subsequent research has supported the same principle: Forgetting takes place most rapidly immediately after learning and then declines more slowly.

How can you avoid or at least reduce the ravages of this very large amount of forgetting, and remember what you have learned over a long-term period of weeks, months, or even years? The answer seems to lie in **spaced reviews** of previously learned material over a period of time rather than **massed reviews** of familiar material coming all about the same time, or, even worse, last-minute cramming of new material.

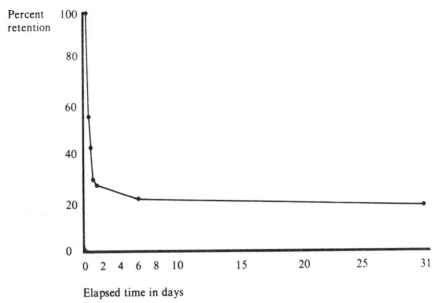

Percent retention

Elapsed time in days

Figure 6.2   Curve of forgetting.
Source: Adapted from the research described by Hermann Ebbinghaus, Memory: A Contribution to Experimental Psychology, *trans. H. A. Ruger and C. E. Bussenius (New York: Teachers College, Columbia University, 1913). (Originally published Leipzig: Altenberg, 1885.)*

Lyon appears to have been the first to recommend an arrangement of spaced review calculated to compensate for the forgetting curve. In general, it was found[2]

> that the most economical method for keeping material once memorized from disappearing, was to review the material whenever it started to "fade." Here also the intervals were found to be, roughly speaking, in arithmetical proportion [as one day, two days, four days, eight days, etc.]. For similar reasons the student is advised to review his "lecture-notes" shortly after taking them, and if possible, to review them again the evening of the same day. Then a lapse of a week or two does not make nearly so much difference. When once he has forgotten so much that the various associations originally made have vanished, a considerable portion of the material is irretrievably lost.

In contrast, massed review involves a person's concentrating on the reviewing activities of repetition, further explanations, extra practice, and going over the previously learned material in the last day or two or even hours before the exam. Cramming, as mentioned earlier, generally involves a person's pulling an "all-nighter" to learn for the first time everything that he or she should have learned earlier during the term.

A great deal of empirical research indicates that you learn more, particularly with tests of learning coming after a delayed period of time, if your

Chapter 6

review activities are distributed over a period of time rather than massed at one time and place. Austin's study is particularly interesting because it offers insights into the comparative effectiveness of spaced review, massed review, and cramming.[3]

Austin found that spaced review is generally more effective than massed review with both logical material and nonsense syllables, but the greatest value of spaced review becomes apparent when the student is tested two or four weeks after learning. Surprisingly enough, massed review was found to be as effective as distributed practice for *immediate* recall. Apparently, if a student has *already* learned the material well, a review period that comes immediately before an exam can be as useful as reviewing several times over a longer period of time. The disadvantages of massed review apparently lie in diminished long-term retention after an extended period of time. This is a real problem if you rely solely on massed reviews because you may find yourself having to relearn material that you would have remembered better if you had used a schedule of distributed review.

The problems are even greater with cramming because you are faced with having to learn an abundance of new material all at one time with no opportunity to review. An actor faces a similar situation by trying to learn a part for the first time on the day of the performance: It makes for a bad show! It is possible to cram or study so hard that the work of a whole term, not learned when it was originally assigned, can be retained for 12 or 24 hours. But it takes tremendous effort to cram that much material into your mind in a short period, and, more importantly, anything that you learn in this way you forget almost *immediately*.

Our model of verbal learning explains the superiority of spaced review over massed review, and the superiority of both techniques over cramming. All three techniques require that you pay attention to the material. However, in the case of cramming, you are not likely to have the time or take the time to meaningfully process the words by translating them into internal or external speech and then bringing to mind the meanings of the words. It is even less likely that you will be able to form the essential associative linkages between the new material and what you already know. The superiority of spaced reviews over massed reviews is explained in terms of the encoding and associative linkages that receive greater reinforcement with spaced reviews. Since you go over the material more times, the encoding and linkages do not fade.

Taking Notes on Your Notes

Now that it has been established that it is better to review previously learned material over a period of time than it is to cram, the question arises as to what the best actual review activities are for you to engage in. Recitation has already been discussed as an empirically supported review activity. It appears to be effective in counteracting the forgetting curve. One study compared students who reread information with students who recited the information in their own words immediately after reading it.[4] Seven days later, the reciters remembered 83% of what they read whereas the readers remembered only 33%. This study emphasizes the importance of meaningful encoding.

Another review activity, taking notes on your notes, is a natural outgrowth of the paragraph method discussed earlier in Chapter 5. The paragraph method involves briefly summarizing the contents of each paragraph in your own words. If this method is used throughout the course, three-page or less summaries of each chapter will then be available for you to use in reviewing. It is also recommended that you go through your lecture notes, consolidating them in your own words in a similar way.

When it is time to review for an exam, and ideally this will be done over a period of weeks rather than immediately before an exam, you then review your "paragraph method" notes that you made over the assigned reading and your consolidated lecture notes in order to make "notes on your notes." The purpose is to carefully read through all your existing notes, and to further mentally reorganize, encode, and condense them so that your total amount of notes is further consolidated. The goal is to reduce each of your three pages of paragraph-method reading notes and lecture notes to one page. Figure 6.3 provides an example of taking notes on the notes taken by using the paragraph method in the section on "Films and Filmstrips" in Chapter 4.

You continue the process until you reach the ultimate goal: summarizing all of the most important parts of the material for the exam on both sides of one sheet of notebook paper. Of course, you will not be able to include many ideas and details on the one sheet, but the process of your repeatedly going over the material to consolidate it increases the probability that you will be paying attention to the important aspects of the material, and that the necessary encoding, associative linkages, reviewing, and reorganizing processes will occur.

Taking notes on your notes meets the demands of verbal learning. As one student said after first trying this recommended method, "Taking notes on my notes forces me to do what I should be doing, but can get away without doing when I review by just rereading my notes or the textbook."

Find Out the Kind of Test You Are Taking

Many articles on studying for exams emphasize the importance of finding out what kind of test to expect. Unlike many of the other recommendations in traditional study manuals or articles, this one is research supported. Studies indicate that students perform better on the kind of retention test

The original notes taken by using the paragraph method discussed in the section on "Films and Filmstrips" in chapter 4 are reproduced below.

Paragraph 1. films and filmstrips commonly used in schools but little empirical research on effectiveness

Paragraph 2. clear that students can learn from films if used effectively

Paragraph 3. students learn more if know in advance what important points to look for and if related to course content

Paragraph 4. note taking *can* interfere with learning from films if interferes with paying attention

Paragraph 5. students learn best if concentrate on film while shown, and have study guide before or after film to focus attention

Paragraph 6. taking notes *during* film can interfere too much with important job of paying attention

Below is an example of reducing these notes by a ratio of about three to one so that the notes on the notes are now approximately 1/3 of their original length. The exact form of the notes is not nearly as important as making them personally meaningful to you.

more film learning if related to course, given key points to watch for.
note taking during film can interfere with paying attention; best to concentrate on film, use study guide for key points before or afterwards.

This process can be continued over all the sections of the material you are responsible for learning. Eventually, through the use of this process, you should be able to condense the material for the entire exam on both sides of one sheet of paper.

Figure 6.3   An example of taking notes on the notes.

that they have been led to expect. For example, it was found that students who organized material in anticipation of an essay test (called a *free-recall test*) performed less well on a multiple-choice test (called a *recognition test*).[5] Students apparently use different information from the learning material to pass different kinds of tests. For example, a student's scores on multiple-choice or recognition tests are increased by encoding that concentrates on identifying as many details and characteristics of each item of information as possible so that he or she can recognize each item from many different perspectives and distinguish it from similar kinds of items. On the other hand, the student's essay or recall performance is increased by encoding that emphasizes the ways in which different items of information are associated and interrelated so that he or she can relate one item in many different ways to other items.

To illustrate the distinctions between studying for recall and recognition tests, consider Lincoln's three-part plan for winning the American Civil War. Briefly, Lincoln's plan involved a naval blockade of the Confederacy, gaining control of the Mississippi River in order to cut the Confederacy in two, and capturing Richmond, the capital of the Confederacy. The best way for a student to study this plan for a multiple-choice recognition test would be to learn as much as possible about as many of the details and specifics in each of the three parts so that he or she could identify each step even if it were stated in many different ways. A student who is studying for an essay recall test would be better advised to emphasize the similarities among the three parts of the plan, such as the fact that both the naval blockade and capturing the Mississippi had as their goal the *isolation* of the Confederacy. Then the student can adapt the information that he or she learns to answer any related question that might be asked.

There are several practical implications in these findings. Try to do everything that you can to find out the kind of test you will be given. Suggested activities include asking the instructor what kind of test will be given and, from the instructor's perspective, what the key issues and key approaches to the subject are. Also consult any test files that might be available, and talk to the instructor's former students. See Figure 6.4 for a guide to 12 different kinds of tests that may be given.

Taking the Exam

In preparing for and taking exams, it is important to use all of the study techniques discussed earlier in the text such as taking efficient notes by using the paragraph method or key point cards, giving oral summaries of what you have learned, and reviewing rather than cramming. All of these methods are associated with increased success on tests. There is *no substitute for hard work.* But even after you have thoroughly learned the material, you still need to know how to take a test in an organized, efficient way, that is, you need to have test-wiseness. The following suggestions should be helpful.

To avoid wasting time at the pencil sharpener, you should be sure to take several well-sharpened pencils to an exam. If tests are to be graded by a computer, then you must use a No. 2 pencil.

Read the directions for the exam carefully. Most directions say to choose the **best answer.** You should look for the best answer, which is the one that includes the most information that is correct without including anything incorrect. Several options may contain correct information but still not be the *best* alternative. In most tests, the answer that you ordinarily think of as being correct will be the right answer. If you attempt to read your personal interpretations into the question, you are very likely to answer it incorrectly.

Figure 6.4 A concise guide to 12 kinds of tests.
Source: Taken from "A Concise Guide to 12 Kinds of Tests" by Don Eastman. Reprinted by permission from the 1978 issue of Insider. *Copyright © 1978 by 13-30 Corporation.*

Demonstration. In lab courses, you may be expected to show the instructor that you can perform certain basic operations, such as preparing a microscope slide. The only way to study for this is to practice the operation regularly in class until you're certain you are doing it correctly.

Essay. The first thing to do on an essay exam is to read each question carefully—watching for words like *explain, compare, describe, analyze, contrast*—and be sure you understand what you're being asked to do. If the question says to *compare* two items, it won't do to simply *describe* them. Then work your way from the easiest questions to the hardest questions, being careful to think through each answer before you write it. An effective technique is to use as many specific names and references as you can.

Fill-in-the-Blank. Sometimes called "completion" exams, such tests require you to provide the correct word or phrase that completes the statement. One way to study for this type of test is to organize the material into definite statements as you go.

Identification. You usually find such tests in the lab sections of science courses. You're shown a collection of specimens which you have to identify and provide information about. The way to prepare is to memorize several distinguishing characteristics for each item. Another type of identification test provides the name of a person or place and asks you to supply as many facts about that person or place as you can.

Matching. The task here is to associate an item on one list with its complement on another list—for instance, matching people's names with their accomplishments, words with definitions, and the like. Obviously, you should first match the items you are most sure of and then, unless there's a penalty for guessing, match the remaining items through the process of elimination. Check the instructions before you start: can any of the "answers" be used more than once?

Multiple Choice. Theoretically such tests should be easy because the answer *is* one of the alternatives, and, through elimination, you should be able to figure out which one. A common mistake that people make is to choose the first statement that seems right without reading the rest—the object of many tests is to choose the *best* answer from more than one correct statement.

Open Book. Most open-book exams are constructed in such a way that you cannot readily find the answer in the textbook. For example, you may be told to analyze the facts or interpret them in some way. Nonetheless, the book may help you recall buzz (certain) words and phrases.

Oral Exams. These are probably the hardest of all exams because most people are better at padding their writing than their speech. Do not attempt to bluff your way through a question that you're not prepared to answer. Instead, when a question is asked, consider for a moment what you *can* talk about with some assurance and then proceed. . . .

Problem Solving. The best way to study for such exams is to work practice problems until you are confident that you understand how to work the formula in all cases. When you finish each problem on the test, recheck each step of the answer to be sure you haven't made a mistake. Then label your answer to help the grader find it.

(cont. on next page)

Figure 6.4 (cont.)

Short Answer. This kind of test requires you to answer each question in several sentences rather than the longer answer that is required on an essay exam. You study for it much as you do for an essay exam.

Take Home. This type of exam is really a series of short themes which you prepare outside of class, using whatever resources you want. Profs usually set a limit on the amount of time you are to spend writing the exam, but students who score high often exceed this time limit considerably. The professor expects you to produce well-crafted answers when you're working with both books and time in the quiet of your own room.

True-False. You read a statement and pronounce it true or false. It's as simple as that. Don't try to interpret a statement too closely—most true-false questions are clearly stated—but do look out for words like *always, never,* or *only* which usually indicate that the statement is false.

The Four-Step Plan

A recommended method for taking an exam involves going through the exam four times.[6]

1. The *first* time through, you should move through the exam quickly, answering all questions about which you are fairly certain. This first time through the exam serves two functions. First, by going through the exam quickly, you can get a fairly large part of it completed without spending too much of the testing time. Second, it is highly likely that by going through the exam quickly you will remember or become aware of answers to questions that you would not otherwise remember. For example, something in question 50 will remind you of or give you the answer to question 15. By going through the test quickly the first time through, you become familiar with its entire content. In order to save time for the remaining three times through the test, it is important to use no more than *half* of the total time for this step. It is a good idea to wear your watch to exams and to keep track of the time as you proceed through the exam.

2. The *second* time through the test is very brief because all you do is go down the test answering those questions you were reminded of or now remember. If you are well prepared, you should now have answered a large part of the exam already, but, no matter how prepared you are, there will still be some unanswered questions. This is where the third step comes in.

3. The purpose of the *third* time through the exam is to complete the entire test. Two rules of thumb are useful here. The general underlying principle of these two rules is that you should *never ever* simply guess, that is, close your eyes and point to the right answer. There are many more effective techniques to use. First, you should attempt to eliminate some of the options as incorrect. If there are four options to a question and you have to purely guess, there is only a 25% (1 out of 4) chance of getting it right. If you can eliminate one option as wrong and then still have to guess, the chances are 33⅓% (or 1 out of 3) of getting it right. If two options can be

eliminated, the chances of getting it right by guessing have improved to 50% (1 out of 2). Thus you should take advantage of the mathematics of the situation.

Second, if you have eliminated some of the options as incorrect but still do not know the correct answer, there are still better ways to answer the question than through pure guesswork. Assume that you are a student unfamiliar with American history and are faced with this question that you are not able to answer the first or second time through the exam.

Who was the first President of the United States?
a. Thomas Jefferson
b. George Washington
c. Donald Duck
d. Al Capone

Using the first rule of thumb discussed above, you should eliminate any options that you know are wrong rather than simply guess. It will be assumed that you are able to eliminate option 3 because you are familiar with cartoon characters, and you are able to eliminate option 4 because you know about famous gangsters. Now your chances of getting the question right through purely guessing which alternative is correct have improved to 50%. Options 3 and 4 may appear absurd, but in many actual test questions one or two of the options may be no more ridiculous in their context that options 3 and 4, therefore, they can easily be eliminated.

Now you are down to two options and this is where the second rule of thumb becomes helpful. First, you can choose the answer that you initially thought of as being correct, unless upon your further evaluation and reading of the test you have now come up with a good reason why the answer that you first selected as correct is really incorrect. If you never had any notion at all of the correct answer, then you are advised to choose the second option if you have not already eliminated it. Note that the example above was "rigged" to illustrate the value of this rule of thumb! However, it is not just wild advise to choose the second option because it can be justified for two basic reasons.[7] First, it gives you a rule of thumb that you can use to answer questions when you have no notion of the correct answer. This helps to eliminate the anxiety that results from trial-and-error behavior in such cases. Second, there is sometimes a tendency on the part of the test maker in listing the choices to make the first choice a seductive alternative and the second choice the right answer.

4. By the end of the third time through the test, you should have answered all questions. This is where some students give up (or run out of time if they have not watched the time carefully), but if you are willing to hang in there and go through the test the *fourth* time through, you are most likely to maximize your score. It is recommended that you go through the exam completely again to double-check the questions to make certain that they still read the way they first appeared to, to check your answers to make certain that they are the ones that you still think are correct, and to make certain you made no clerical errors in filling out the answer sheet. This is

1. Go through the test fairly quickly answering all the questions that are readily apparent, using no more than half of the total available time.

2. Go through the test a second time answering all the questions you have now remembered.

3. Answer all the rest of the questions the third time through by first eliminating the alternatives that you know are incorrect, and then by selecting either the answer you first thought of as right or the second alternative if you did not previously eliminate it.

4. Use the fourth time through the test to double-check that you *actually* answered all the questions in the way that you intended.

Figure 6.5   Summary of four-step plan for taking an exam.

the time you will most likely catch the "dumb" mistakes that you are likely to kick yourself for later, for example, missing the *not* in a question, or mentally reading in a *not* that is not really there. Probably the best way to go through the test the fourth time is to cover up the answer sheet with your hand or a blank sheet of paper and reread each question. Mentally determine the answer once again, then uncover the answer sheet to see if this was the answer that you previously recorded. If so, you have double assurance that your answer is correct. If not, then you need to rethink the question and correct answer.

In summary, the four-step plan for taking the exam described above will improve your chances for increasing your score because each time that you go through the test you have a different purpose. Putting all four purposes together helps you to eliminate possible sources of error on an exam. Figure 6.5 provides a concise summary of this four-step plan for taking an exam.

To Change or Not to Change Answers

One further point should be noted. There is a common misperception among students that they should never change answers because they usually change them from right to wrong. However, several studies have revealed that students are significantly more likely to change their answers from wrong to right than from right to wrong.[8]

By studying your returned tests, you can determine your individual tendencies to change answers from right to wrong or from wrong to right. Keep a sheet of paper in your notebook with two columns labeled "Right to Wrong" and "Wrong to Right," and keep track of these changes as tests are returned in several courses over an academic term. At the end of the term, add up the numbers in each column in order to determine which course of action is probably personally best for you. Using this method will be most helpful to you in those cases where it is a real tossup whether the answer you are considering changing is right or not. On the other hand, if you feel more strongly that the option you originally selected is correct or incorrect, then you are probably better off staying with your original answer or changing it regardless of what the calculations from your columns indicate.

Coaching versus Cramming for Standardized Tests

Standardized tests such as the Scholastic Aptitude Test (SAT), the Law School Aptitude Test (LSAT), and the Graduate Record Exam (GRE) have been used for many years to predict success in college, law school, or graduate school. Even though you already may have taken the SAT and have no immediate plans for taking a standardized test like the LSAT or GRE, the material that is presented in this section will provide you with useful background on preparing for any future standardized test that you might take. This section also serves as a helpful review of the practical implications of the spaced review versus cramming distinctions, which were discussed earlier in this chapter.

Until recently the Educational Testing Service, which administers and develops standardized tests, and the College Board, responsible for the SAT, have consistently maintained that these tests measure student abilities developed over a lifetime and that student test scores are, therefore, not susceptible to short-term attempts to improve them. Thus, in the past, it was argued that tests such as the SAT and GRE measure raw abilities that are not influenced by coaching.

Specifically, in regard to the SAT, the College Board published a booklet in 1968, which was still being distributed recently, that defined *coaching* as "a variety of methods used in attempting to increase in a relatively short time students' mastery of the particular skills, concepts, and reasoning abilities tested by the SAT."[9] The term "relatively short time" was not defined, but, judging from the rest of the booklet, it appeared to be as long as a few weeks or months of tutoring. According to the booklet, past research on coaching indicated that gains in scores were consistently small regardless of which coaching method was used, and the gains did not warrant the time, effort, and expense involved.

However, a research report (1979) from the Federal Trade Commission's Bureau of Consumer Protection on the effects of coaching for the SAT contradicts, at least to some degree, the earlier positions of the College Board and Educational Testing Service. According to this report, "coaching" may help certain students improve their scores on both the mathematical and verbal sections of the SAT. Albert Kramer, head of the Consumer Bureau, was quoted as saying, "A class of students described as 'underachievers' might be helped by coaching to improve their test scores by an average of 25 points on both the verbal and mathematical portions of the SAT."[10] *Underachievers* are defined as students who do not score as well on the SAT as would be expected from their school grades and other personal characteristics.

The Federal Trade Commission's report has been criticized for a variety of errors in the design and analysis of the study. The effects of coaching on LSAT scores were also studied, but the Consumer Bureau's report did not release the results. The Federal Trade Commission said it has "reached no final conclusion as to whether commercial coaching is a desirable alternative for students."[11]

The conflicting results obtained by the College Board and the Educational Testing Service and by the Federal Trade Commission may be explained at least partially by different definitions of cramming and coaching. The Educational Testing Service and the College Board now appear to be arguing that there is a difference between cramming, which involves very short-term intensive *drills* on sample test questions, and coaching, which involves longer-term *instruction* in mathematical and verbal skills.[12] The former is a waste of time whereas it is possible that the latter may help some students.

The Stanley H. Kaplan Educational Center provides a good example of a commercial coaching school, but there are many other commercial programs available. It was one of the two coaching schools studied in the Federal Trade Commission's report, and the only one found to have some effect on raising scores. The Kaplan program for SAT test preparation consists of four 10-hour class sessions, home-study materials, and 200 additional hours of sample tests and taped materials. Kaplan himself has been quoted as saying that cramming for the SAT is not worthwhile.[13] Instead, he provides a long-range program of coaching for the test. Kaplan is adamant, however, that coaching does work because "to make an uncoachable exam is ridiculous. To say you can't improve scores is to say you can't improve students."[14] The Federal Trade Commission study, as discussed above, found an average gain of 25 points for some types of students on both the mathematical and verbal sections of the SAT, which resulted from the Kaplan program.

The distinction between cramming and coaching is reminiscent of the distinction between spaced review and cramming discussed earlier in this chapter. The results of the Federal Trade Commission study are consistent with the empirical research reviewed earlier: Coaching (equivalent to spaced practice) can be effective with at least certain kinds of students. In contrast, cramming, in agreement with the earlier studies of the Educational Testing Service and the College Board, has little or no effect on

SAT scores because longer-term retention is greatly reduced when material is learned too quickly for adequate encoding and associative linkage to occur.

Now, where does all this leave you when you are faced with an upcoming SAT, LSAT, or GRE test?[15] Coaching courses appear to be best suited for underachievers who panic on tests and thus do not do their best. The Federal Trade Commission's study found that underachievers raised their scores an average of 50 points over previous test scores after taking Kaplan's 10-week course. Coaching courses can be very helpful to students who have been out of school for several years and who need to review not only mathematical and verbal subject matter, but also test-wiseness principles such as the use of time during a test, reading test directions, and knowing when and how to guess. Coaching courses are also helpful to students who are attempting to maximize their scores in order to be admitted to a very selective school, and to students who are not likely to be motivated enough to review for a test on their own.

It should be noted that self-instructional review books for standardized tests are also available quite inexpensively from such publishers as Contemporary Books and Barron's Educational Series. Even though the effectiveness of these review books has not been empirically tested, it is possible that they can be as useful as a coaching course. However, you must be well motivated to work through these books on your own. If you decide to use one of these books, be sure to purchase a book that has a recent copyright date.

In selecting the best coaching course, several factors should be considered. A good course, for example, should last over an extended period of 7 to 10 weeks, should have small classes of no more than 30 or 35, and should use up-to-date instructional materials.

In evaluating the evidence about the effects of coaching on standardized test scores, it is important to keep in mind that both sides of the controversy no doubt have their own interests at stake as well as the students' interests. The issue is the extent to which coaching *increases* scores; there is no evidence that indicates that coaching significantly *decreases* scores. Even if coaching only teaches students how to take tests, this in itself may well be worthwhile. Perhaps the Consumer Bureau of the Federal Trade Commission said it best when they asserted in their report, "Even though it cannot be firmly concluded that coaching will work for everyone, the results of the study do show that coaching can be effective for those who do not score well on standardized tests."[16] Students who do not score as well as they would like on standardized tests (and who does not fall into that category except the rare person with a perfect score) might be well advised to consider a coaching course or a do-it-yourself review book.

Exercises

Note: Chapter 7 will provide suggestions for taking an essay exam. At the end of that chapter, you will be given a practice test containing both multiple-choice and essay questions so that you can practice the suggestions for test-wiseness given in this chapter and Chapter 7.

1. In the section on "Preparing for Examinations," you were advised to review rather than cram for examinations, to take notes on your notes as part of the reviewing process, and to find out the kind of test that you will be taking. You might find it helpful to reread these sections before completing this exercise.

   Select an exam that you will be taking in the near future. In the spaces below, write your specific plans for carrying out these three kinds of advice. For example, under the section for reviewing rather than cramming, you might write that you have scheduled yourself to study two hours every night for the exam during the two weeks preceding the test. Under the section for finding out the kind of test you will be taking, you might write that you have already checked with the instructor of the course. She said that the exam will have multiple-choice and short-answer questions.

   a. *This is my plan for reviewing rather than cramming for the exam:*

   b. *These are my plans for taking notes on my notes:*

   c. *This is how I plan to find out about the kind of test that I will be taking:*

Continue to practice filling out this form for your exams for other courses as they are scheduled.

Notes

1. Hermann Ebbinghaus, *Memory: A Contribution to Experimental Psychology,* trans. H. A. Ruger and C. E. Bussenius (New York: Teachers College, Columbia University, 1913). (Originally published Leipzig: Altenberg, 1885.)
2. Darwin Oliver Lyon, "The Optimal Distribution of Time, and the Relation of Length of Material to Time Taken for Learning," *The Journal of Philosophy, Psychology and Scientific Methods* IX (1912): 386.

3. See, for example, Sarah D. MacKay Austin, "A Study in Logical Memory," *American Journal of Psychology* XXXII (1932): 370–403; or Ernst Z. Rothkopf and Esther U. Coke, "Repetition Interval and Rehearsal Method in Learning Equivalences for Written Sentences," *Journal of Verbal Learning and Verbal Behavior* II (1963): 406–416.

4. Herbert F. Spitzer, "Studies in Retention," *Journal of Educational Psychology* XXX (1939): 641–656.

5. Barbara Tversky, "Encoding Processes in Recognition and Recall," *Cognitive Psychology* V (1973): 275–287.

6. This four-part method for taking an examination is based on the suggestions given by Wilbert J. McKeachie in *Teaching Tips: A Guidebook for the Beginning College Teacher* (Lexington, MA: D.C. Heath, 1969), pp. 133–135. For more detailed information on test-wiseness, see also, Rudolph E. Sarnacki, "An Examination of Test-Wiseness in the Cognitive Test Domain," *Review of Educational Research* IL (1979): 252–279.

7. McKeachie.

8. Derek Vidler and Richard Hansen, "Answer-Changing on Multiple Choice Tests," *Journal of Experimental Education* IL (1980): 18–20.

9. College Board booklet quoted by Robert L. Jacobson, "Can 'Coaching' Help Students Score Higher on the S.A.T.'s?" *The Chronicle of Higher Education,* April 16, 1979, p. 9.

10. Albert Kramer quoted in Cheryl M. Fields, " 'Coaching' Courses May Help Some Students Increase SAT Scores, Study Concludes," *The Chronicle of High Education,* June 18, 1979, p. 3.

11. Federal Trade Commission quoted in "FTC Takes A Second Look at Coaching Study," *ETS Developments* XXVI (1979): 8.

12. Robert L. Jacobson, "ETS Concedes Special Preparation Can Boost Test Scores," *The Chronicle of Higher Education,* September 15, 1980, p. 13.

13. Stanley Kaplan quoted in Jacobson.

14. Stanley Kaplan quoted in Carrie Tuhy, "Does College-Board Coaching Make the Grade?" *Money,* October 1979, p. 108.

15. Tuhy.

16. Consumer Bureau of the Federal Trade Commission quoted in Fields.

Writing Course Papers and Essay Exams　　7

Objectives

You will learn how to prepare for and write course papers.
You will learn how to take essay tests.

Key Terms

proposal

dumping papers

proofreading

plagiarism

footnote

thesis

Overview: The Importance of Writing Well

College-bound and college students are expected to be able to write well.[1] They should be able to write clear, grammatical sentences, and to be able to organize these sentences to develop and clearly express an idea or theme. Instructors frequently use course papers and essay exams in order to provide practice in writing, to assess present writing ability, and to test what the student has learned. This chapter will provide you with some practical help in writing good course papers and exams.

Writing Course Papers

A review of the literature reveals that research studies on the best way to write course papers appear to be nonexistent. Many people have opinions on how to write good course papers, but they remain just that—opinions—until they are experimentally validated. However, writing papers is an important part of students' lives, and some advice would be helpful to many of them. Therefore, this section consists of a summary of suggestions for writing good papers that experts on writing have offered. You should keep in mind, however, that unlike many preceding sections of this text, there will be no references to experimental support for the effectiveness of these suggestions.

Instructors assign course papers for three basic reasons.[2] The writing of course papers helps students go beyond what is ordinarily covered in the course, and they are able to become somewhat of an expert in a limited related area. Through the writing of papers, students may learn something about the actual process of accumulating knowledge. Writing papers also helps students to individualize a course by investigating topics of particular interest, which may increase their motivation.

According to writing specialists, there are nine essential steps involved in writing a good term paper. Faithfully following the nine steps below may prove helpful in combating the common student feeling that writing a term paper is the worst part of a course. Again, these suggestions are for the most part not experimentally validated, but they do result from writing instructors' and their students' actual experiences.

1. *Choose a topic.* First, go over assigned or suggested readings and look for an idea or subject that really interests you. Then ask yourself three questions— "What?" "Why?" "How?"—to help you narrow it down. If you're writing a paper for a marine biology class, for example, and you're interested in water pollution, you might ask, "What area of the country has the highest water pollution rate and why?" and "How does it affect fish and plant life in a particular body of water?" Find out the general answers to your questions, then write down exactly what you intend to do—solve a problem, explain a situation, take a position on an issue—says Dr. Rosemary Hake, a Chicago State University English professor who has developed writing programs at eight colleges. Then list the points that you plan to develop more fully in your paper.

2. *Write a proposal.* One way to ensure that you don't get a poor grade because you didn't follow the assignment or because you went off the track is to write and submit a **proposal** to your professor five or six weeks before the paper is due. Your proposal should be only a page or two long, and you should put only a maximum of five hours' work into it. It should contain a tentative introduction. If you're having trouble writing one, break down what you want to say into major steps, reasons, explanations, types, aspects— whatever categories best fit your topic—and write your introduction from that. Your proposal should also mention the sources you plan to use. The best place to start is with your course bibliography and books mentioned at the end of textbook chapters. Your school librarian can give you ideas about other books or journals. Talk over your proposal with your professor to be sure you're on the right track.

3. *Research your information.* Before you actually begin to take notes, be sure to outline the major points you're going to include in your paper to save yourself work that doesn't relate to your paper. Professor Hake advises her students to create what she calls **dumping papers**—sheets which cover

each of the major points. You might use a numbering or lettering system, or different colored paper to identify each dumping paper. Then as you do your research, copy information onto the appropriate sheet.

It's not necessary to copy everything verbatim; it saves time to paraphrase unless you intend to quote the material later. In either case, be sure you copy all the relevant information (title, author, page number, volume, etc.) so that you don't have to go back to look it up if you decide to footnote that information. You don't have to read entire books to get material you need; scan tables of contents and chapter introductions, section headings and summaries.

Overresearching is a big problem for most students; you should devote roughly one-third of your total work time to research, says Professor Nold.

4. *Analyze your findings.* Your term paper shouldn't be simply a summary of facts or other people's criticisms about your topic; it should also reflect critical thinking on your part, say Frederick Turner and Ronald Sharp, professors of English at Kenyon College and coeditors of the *Kenyon Review,* a literary quarterly. Some students begin to focus and arrange their thoughts about what they're going to write as they research—either mentally or by writing down their comments next to ones they copy from sources. Other students don't actually start putting their thoughts on paper until they start writing their first draft. Either method is fine, but if you analyze as you research, you should spend less time on your first draft and vice versa. Your analysis and first draft together should make up another third of your total work time.

5. *Write a first draft.* Most professors say that content and organization are more important than how the paper is written. The best place to start— assuming your introduction is written and revised if necessary—is by writing several paragraphs for each of your main points. You can then decide whether you need to add or delete information. Try to put your thoughts in your own words rather than relying on how other authors phrased theirs. And don't overuse quotes. "They should be used the way a drunk uses a lamppost—for support and illumination," says Professor Turner.

Heavily footnoted papers are more likely to receive higher grades because it looks as though you've put more work into the paper, but using quotes that add nothing to the point you're making won't help. Avoid misusing big words; studies have found that professors do give higher grades to papers that contain flowery language, but unless you know how to use a word properly, it will work against you.

6. *Edit your first draft.* Put yourself in your professor's shoes and go over your paper to make sure it flows well; that is, each paragraph makes sense, each paragraph connects with the one preceding and following it, and all paragraphs logically proceed from the introduction to the conclusion. Professor Hake suggests asking yourself the following editing questions: Would the paragraph make sense if it were broken down into more than one? Does it need more detail, explanation or examples? What is the point of the paragraph? Are the sentences in logical order? Does each sentence say what you want it to?

Don't be afraid to cut and paste; this is the time to reorganize any sentences or paragraphs that make more sense somewhere else and to delete extraneous material—if it looks padded to you, the professor is sure to notice it, too.

7. *Proofread your paper.* Read each sentence for grammar, punctuation and structure, as well as typographical errors.

8. *Have a friend critique your paper.* Everyone, even distinguished authors, needs an editor. Ask someone in your class, a roommate, a friend (preferably someone who is a good writer) to read your paper. Ask him or her to mark anything that is unclear, excessive, poorly stated or grammatically incorrect.

9. *Write a final draft.* Rewrite the sentences or paragraphs that your reader had difficulty with and show him or her your revised version to make sure you've corrected the difficulty. If you have time, put your paper aside for a few days and edit it one more time before you write and type your final draft. Most professors say that the way the paper looks is the least important factor in grading, but it certainly is a plus to have it neatly typed.[3]

Postscript on Plagiarism

A postscript about plagiarism appears to be in order here. **Plagiarism** involves the stealing or use of other authors' direct words or their ideas or substance without crediting the source.

Direct stealing of authors' words sometimes occurs, of course, when a student who is frantic to finish a paper by the next day sits down and copies word for word something that another person has written. Experienced teachers usually have little difficulty spotting the plagarized papers, especially if the instructor happens to be the *actual* author of the material that the student is trying to pass off as his or her own, which is something that has actually happened!

A much more likely occurrence, however, is plagiarism that happens because the student does not understand how to use source material in the accepted scholarly way.[4] In writing a course paper, a student may borrow either the actual words of the reference (quoting) or may restate the idea of the reference in his or her own words (paraphrasing). *Both* uses of other people's words and ideas require a **footnote** of acknowledgment. Consult the instructor of your course for the proper form for these footnotes or references.

Many students appear to slip into plagiarism through the back door by taking sloppy reading notes. They write down ideas from their references as they read and may neglect to put in the quotation marks that indicate these words are a direct quote. Then when the students use these words in their paper, they believe they have restated the ideas in their own words since there are no quotation marks on their note card, but, in reality, they are copying a direct quotation into their paper. This is why it is essential for you to use quotation marks around anything that is a direct quote, which you have written on note cards. Be sure also to copy down the complete reference and to check the quotation word for word for accuracy against the original. Then it is possible to be sure that you are giving credit where credit is due.

Pauk has eloquently stated the case for accurate documentation in course papers in this way:

> Abundant and conscientious documentation in a research paper is not a confession of lack of originality. The more thorough and scholarly the treatment of a topic, the more exhaustive is the search into and use of sources. Originality lies in the use you make of your findings, in your thinking about them, your interpretation of them, the connections you make and the conclusions you draw. This part of the paper is your own. You use and cite sources, in other words, as evidence to substantiate *your* development of *your* **thesis.**[5]

A Final Checklist

Once you have written a course paper following all the suggestions given above, it is still an excellent idea to give the paper one final check. A good way to do this is by using the "Final Checklist for Evaluating Course Papers" provided in Figure 7.1. This checklist helps you to focus on the specifics involved in the three essential elements of Content, Organization, and Style and Mechanics when you are editing your paper. You can often get an idea of how your paper might be graded as a result of the number of affirmative answers you can give yourself in response to these questions. You can also use this checklist to evaluate another student's paper.

One final word of advice is to read the paper *out loud* to yourself before submitting it. The ear can often pick up mistakes overlooked by the eye.

Special Suggestions for Taking Essay Tests

Many of the suggestions given in Chapter 6 for taking multiple-choice tests also apply to essay tests. You should begin an essay test by reading through all the questions in order to get an idea of what is expected so that you can budget your time accordingly. Be sure that you understand what the question is asking. If the question asks you to "list the causes," be sure to provide a *list* rather than "describe the causes" or "discuss the causes." It is important to know the meanings of common test words such as relate or describe. Figure 7.2 provides useful definitions for some of the common vocabulary of test taking. It is important to answer the question *exactly* as it is stated and not in terms of what the question *may* be asking or what *you think* the question should ask.

I. *Content:* Is the conception clear, accurate, and perceptive?
  A. Is the subject matter discussed intelligently?
    1. Does the paper display adequate knowledge of the subject matter?
    2. Are there any penetrating insights or fresh perceptions?
    3. Are errors in logic avoided?
  B. Does the essay offer evidence in support of generalizations?
II. *Organization:* Is the method of presentation clear, effective, and interesting?
  A. Is it possible to state clearly the central idea of the essay?
  B. Is the central idea of the paper as a whole sufficiently developed through the use of details and examples?
  C. Are the individual paragraphs sufficiently developed?
  D. Are all the ideas of the essay relevant?
  E. Are the ideas developed in logical order?
    1. Are the paragraphs placed in natural and logical sequence within the whole?
    2. Are the sentences placed in natural and logical sequence within the paragraphs?
  F. Are the transitions adequate?
  G. Are the ideas given the emphasis required by their importance?
  H. Is the point of view consistent and appropriate?
III. *Style and Mechanics:* Does the essay observe standards of style and mechanics generally accepted by educated writers?
  A. Are the sentences clear and grammatically correct? (For example, are they reasonably free of fragments, run-on sentences, comma splices, faulty parallel structure, mixed constructions, dangling modifiers, and errors of agreement, case, and verb forms?)
  B. Is the sentence structure effective?
    1. Is there appropriate variety in sentence structure?
    2. Are uses of subordination and coordination appropriate?
  C. Is conventional punctuation followed?
  D. Is the spelling correct?
  E. Is the vocabulary accurate, appropriate, and sufficiently varied?
  F. Is the style reasonably concise and free of unnecessary wordiness or "dead wood"?

Figure 7.1 Final checklist for evaluating course papers.
Source: Adapted from a handout for composition students that was kindly provided by David Andersen, one of the manuscript reviewers.

It cannot be stressed too much how important it is to *organize* the contents of an essay answer *before* actually starting to write. If you start to write with the first point that comes to mind followed by any other ideas as you remember them, then you are going to have a badly organized answer. It will be difficult for the instructor to score, and can well result in a lowered grade.

The table below outlines the various categories of test terms, tells you the type of answer that is needed, and then gives examples of specific terms that fit into each category.

General Category	Answer Needed	Examples of Specific Terms
Identification	Present the bare facts: a date, a name, a phrase; in short, provide a concise answer.	cite, define, enumerate, give, identify, indicate, list, mention, name, state
Description	Tell about a specific topic with a certain amount of detail.	describe, discuss, review, summarize, diagram, illustrate, sketch, develop, outline, trace
Relation	Describe the similarities, differences, or associations between two or more subjects.	analyze, compare, contrast, differentiate, distinguish, relate
Demonstration	Show (not state) why something is true or false. Put forth logical evidence or arguments to support a specific statement.	demonstrate, explain why, justify, prove, show, support
Evaluation	Give your opinion or judgment on a subject plus justify and support it. Also, if your opinion can be challenged, be sure to present both sides.	assess, comment, criticize, evaluate, interpret, propose

Figure 7.2   The vocabulary of essay test taking.
Source: The definitions of answers needed and examples of specific terms are adapted from Jason Millman and Walter Pauk, How to Take Tests *(New York: McGraw-Hill, 1969), pp. 152-57. Used with permission. The form of figure 7.2 itself is taken from "The Vocabulary of Test-Taking." Reprinted by permission from the 1975/76 issue of* Nutshell *(Copyright © 1975 by 13-30 Corporation.)*

The best way to organize your answer in advance is to jot down the key points that you wish to cover in the order in which you want to cover them. Then, writing the essay only involves discussing and expanding on the points in the order in which you listed them in your outline.

There are three parts to a good essay answer. The essay should begin with an opening thesis paragraph, sentence, or sentences that state the problem. This introductory section helps to organize the rest of the answer. All essays should end with a concluding paragraph, sentence, or sentences that summarize how the problem was dealt with in a significant way in the essay. In between the opening and concluding sections comes the supporting material in which the introductory problem is supported with specific examples, related to other problems, and is discussed in terms of exceptions or interest implications.

It is just as important to double-check essay exams as multiple-choice exams. Often you can raise your grade by correcting errors, adding missing words, or rewriting an unclear sentence during the last time through the exam. It is important for you to check to see that you actually wrote what you thought you wrote. Errors are easier to correct now than to try to talk the examiner into believing what you really meant to write.

Pauk asked a history professor to describe the errors most commonly made on history exams. The professor's response is very beneficial and applicable to exams in many other kinds of courses as well as to history exams:

Many students fail . . . to label historical movements. They do not state the "time frame." They give no idea whether the movement extended over decades or centuries. We don't insist on exact dates, but we do want to know what the "time slice" is.

Again, many students remain on the general level. I tell my students in class, "Nail down generalities with examples." Even after such a warning, I receive papers without a specific, concrete name of a person, group, or geographical location.

Some students, on the other hand, fill a booklet with facts, but never give the *why* of it at all. What good are the facts if they don't know what the facts stand for?

Though we warn students about illegible writing, we keep right on getting papers that are almost unreadable. This may be incidental, as far as knowledge is concerned, but it affects grades just the same. Yes, I try to understand a scribbled word here and there. I try to make out some words from context. But to ponder, decipher, and guess is not part of the job. If the student knows the answer, it is *his* job to write it so that I can read it. Scribbling is downright rude and inconsiderate.

We want a well-organized essay. We urge the students to start with a thesis. We suggest that they make a brief outline on the inside front cover of the test booklet as an aid to organizing their thoughts and to make the thesis sentence meaningful. But what do we get? A stream-of-consciousness answer.

As I read some of the answers, I find myself muttering, "What does the question ask? . . . Well, then, answer it!" I always suspect an answer which is off-focus. When a student doesn't know much about the question, he often slips to either side of it, into an area about which he knows a little bit more. Then he lays it on, thinking that a mountain of facts will obscure his shift off the topic.

Actually, all a student needs to do is to know his subject cold, read the question carefully, make a slim outline, start off with a topic sentence, and then support it—and I mean *support* it. That's all there is to it.[6]

Summary and Examples

Based on the discussion above, the three basic steps involved in writing a good essay answer can be summarized in this way:

1. Know the subject matter thoroughly.
2. Read the question carefully and organize your answer *before* beginning to write.
3. A well-organized answer should begin with an opening topic section, then present supporting material, and end with a concluding section.

Figure 7.3 presents an example of an essay question on the article "Glaciers," which appears in Chapter 3. The goal of this kind of question is to require the student to build on the information given in the article rather than to just repeat the material exactly as it was given. Five different sample answers scored as being worth from zero to four points are given as examples. As you read the five answers, note how greatly they differ in terms of meeting the demands of the three steps to writing a good essay answer summarized in the previous paragraph.

Figure 7.3   Sample answers to an essay question.
Source: This question, the examples of answers scored from zero to four points, and the illustration were adapted from Russell P. Kropp, Howard W. Stoker, and Louis Bashaw, "The Construction and Validation of Tests of the Cognitive Processes as Described in the 'Taxonomy of Educational Objectives,' " (United States Office of Education Contract OE-4-10-019) (Tallahassee: Florida State University, 1966). Used with permission. The question and sample answers were based on the information contained in the article "Glaciers" by William O. Fields, Scientific American, September 1955, pp. 84-92.

Question on the "Glaciers" article, which appeared earlier in chapter 3:

> The land over which a glacier has passed suffers considerable damage. Briefly outline why glaciers cause damage and describe the kinds of damage they might cause.

Objective of the question:

   The objective of this item is to require students to build upon the implications in the article. The best and more complete answer will go beyond the obvious solution that the glacier will cause much damage due to its large mass. The ideal answer should include a discussion of such things as topological damage, climatic changes, destruction of plant and animal life, and the like.

   This question is worth a total of four points. Below you will find samples of actual students' answers to this question which were scored as worth from zero to four points. Note that as the sample answers move from zero toward four points, they contain more information and become better organized with a clear opening topic sentence, supporting materials, and a concluding section.

Example of an Answer Scored Zero Points

> Everything in the path of the glacier is torn down or smashed because of the weight of the glacier. The weight just crushes everything, all the trees and anything in its path.

This answer only briefly discusses one effect of glaciers—the effects of their large mass.

Example of an Answer Scored One Point

> The weight of the glacier can change the contours of the land a great deal, by flattening hills and forests, filling in crevices and forming lakes. Also, a glacier carries material along with it which it deposits along the way.

(cont. on next page)

Figure 7.3 (cont.)

This answer also concentrates on the effects of the large mass of a glacier, but it does include a brief mention of changes in the topology of the land after a glacier passes.

Example of an Answer Scored Two Points

Glaciers are large, heavy, moving pieces of ice. For this reason, they can cut trenches in ground, ruin crops, carry away soil, and even move large boulders. When the glaciers melt they cause the formation of lakes, rivers, and ponds.

This answer provides some mention of the effects of a glacier on crops and land topology, as well as discussing the effects of the large glacier mass in more detail than the answer above scored as worth one point.

Example of an Answer Scored Three Points

Glaciers weigh a considerable amount. Moving so slowly over land, it could cause ruin to plants and top soil. The run-off could flood a valley and kill animals. A glacier might go to a city or town and destroy millions of dollars worth of property and homes. It would take the land years to grow and mature enough to be able to cultivate or for grazing land, or just for plain forest area.

This answer includes a discussion of the effects of the large mass of a glacier on land topology, and plant, animal, and human life in more detail than the sample answers above. However, the answer is not as well organized as the answer scored four points below because it lacks the structure of an opening topic sentence, supporting materials, and a conclusion.

Example of an Answer Scored Four Points

opening sentence:

Glaciers eliminate all life, both during and after passage.

supporting materials:
The climate conditions associated with glacier formation make it virtually impossible for plant and animal life to survive prior to glacier passage. The bulk and tremendous weight of the glacier removes the top-soil and humus, making it impossible for the ground to sustain vegetation. Erosion is a problem both before and after a glacier, due to this destruction of vegetation.

conclusion:
It takes nature hundreds of years to replace what it lost and sometimes this is never accomplished.

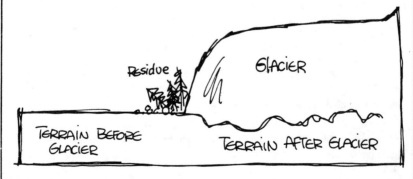

This answer includes discussions and a diagram explaining the effect of the large glacier mass on climate, and topology, soil, and plant and animal life. It is also very well organized with an opening topic sentence, supporting materials, and a concluding sentence on how long it will take to replace what is lost in a glacier.

Exercises

To give you practice in answering multiple-choice and essay questions by using the suggestions for taking these kinds of tests given in Chapters 6 and 7, a short test follows. The test is based on the article on behavior modification given for Exercise 3 of Chapter 4. You might want to reread the article before attempting to answer the questions as well as reread the suggestions for taking multiple-choice and essay exams. Be sure to practice going through the test four times with a different purpose each time through. The key for the exam is given following the test.

Test on "Behavior Modification" Reading from Chapter 4

Directions for Multiple-Choice Questions: Choose the BEST answer.

1. What is the underlying principle of behavior modification?
   a. punishment of the child's existing behavior
   b. unconditional positive regard for the child by the parent
   c. intensive training in alternative, more socially acceptable behavior
   d. positive reinforcement of acceptable behavior

2. Susie did not get along well with her classmates. A therapist came to Susie's class, showed all the children a "Susie box," and told them it would buzz whenever Susie did something particularly good. Each time the box buzzed, Susie and all of her classmates got additional recess time. Changing behavior in such a purposeful way is called:
   a. evaluation
   b. classical conditioning
   c. behavior modification
   d. pinpointing

3. When Miss Starr recorded the occurrence of Paul's disturbances in order to pinpoint the source of his behavior problem, how many disturbances a day did she find that he averaged?
   a. 10
   b. 18
   c. 23
   d. 35

4. According to behavior modification theorists, which of the following actions is the *least* desirable on the part of the teacher or parent?
   a. reward undesirable behavior
   b. disapprove undesirable behavior
   c. ignore undesirable behavior
   d. none of the above

5. Which of the following statements is *incorrect* according to behavior modification theory?
   a. The cause of the problem behavior is unimportant.
   b. Behavior is learned as a result of being associated with pleasant experiences.
   c. Emphasis should be placed on observable pieces of behavior.
   d. It is necessary to change the learner's attitude or basic personality.
6. Which of the following statements is *correct* according to behavior modification theory?
   a. It is impossible to maintain contradictory responses.
   b. Extrinsic rewards should never be used.
   c. It is easier to think yourself into a new way of acting than to act yourself into a new way of thinking.
   d. Ignored behavior usually disappears immediately.
7. The key to the success of behavior modification techniques is
   a. the use of praise
   b. the cooperation of the subject
   c. locating the most effective reinforcer or reward
   d. the use of punishment
8. In behavior modification therapy,
   a. both directive and nondirective approaches are possible
   b. unlearning old habits and learning new ones are the main concerns
   c. the techniques are older and somewhat more acceptable than play, group, or family therapies
   d. the cause, not the symptoms, is treated
9. In behavior modification, reinforcement with a pleasant consequence
   a. elicits the response
   b. is always negative
   c. follows the response
   d. stimulates the reflex
10. The principle involving the experimenter gradually shaping the desired response through the careful use of reinforcement is called
    a. extinction
    b. successive approximations
    c. discrimination
    d. indirect conditioning

Essay Questions:

11. List and briefly describe the four basic steps of behavior modification.

12. In her work with Paul, Miss Starr made use of three basic learning steps. List the three steps and briefly describe each one.

13. How do behavior modification theorists define a *reward?*

14. According to behavior modification theorists, why do we behave the way that we do?

15. Probably the trickiest part of behavior modification therapy is to continue the desirable behavior after the extrinsic reinforcement has been phased out. What method of accomplishing this do experts in behavior modification recommend?

Key for Multiple-Choice Questions:

1. d
2. c
3. c
4. b
5. d
6. a
7. a
8. b
9. c
10. b

Answers for Essay Questions:

11. The four basic steps of behavior modification are:
    a. *Pinpoint* the behavior you want.
    b. *Record* baseline frequency of behavior.
    c. *Consequate* by providing rewards for desired behavior.
    d. *Evaluate* the effect of program; ignored behavior often worsens before it disappears.

12. The three basic learning steps:
    a. structured environment so Paul would *experience* good behavior
    b. helped Paul *discriminate* by rewarding good behavior and ignoring or disapproving undesired behavior
    c. helped Paul *associate* good behavior with reward
13. A *reward* is defined as:
    anything a person will work for.
14. According to behavior modification theorists we act the way we do because:
    our behavior has been associated with pleasant experiences.
15. According to behavior modification therapists, the best way to continue desirable behavior after the extrinsic reinforcement has been phased out is to:
    gradually phase out the tangible reward and replace it with rewards that occur naturally in the environment such as teacher or parent praise.

Notes

1. See, for example, Jack McCurdy, "California Professors Recommend Program to Improve Skills of College-Bound Students," *The Chronicle of Higher Education,* December 2, 1981, p. 6.
2. Wilbert J. McKeachie, *Teaching Tips: A Guidebook for the Beginning College Teacher* (Lexington, MA: D. C. Heath, 1969), p. 122.
3. Reprinted with permission from "9 Steps to Writing the Best Term Paper Ever," by Peggy Schmidt, *Glamour,* May 1979, pp. 354, 356, 358. Courtesy GLAMOUR, Copyright © 1979 by the Condé Nast Publications Inc.
4. Walter Pauk, *How to Study in College* (Boston: Houghton Mifflin, 1962), pp. 94-95.
5. Pauk, p. 95.
6. Walter Pauk: *How to Study in College,* pp. 83, 85. Copyright © 1962 by Houghton Mifflin Company. Reprinted with permission.

Putting It All Together: Developing a Personal Study Plan 8

Objectives

You will review the material that was covered in the last seven chapters.

You will learn how to develop your own personal study plan based on the study techniques discussed in this book.

Overview: How This Chapter Can Help You Develop Your Own Personal Study Plan

A great deal of information about effective study techniques has been presented throughout this book. The purpose of this chapter is to summarize those study techniques by providing a list of practical suggestions for you to use in (a) developing a plan for efficient study, (b) selecting effective study techniques for books, lectures, and films, and finally (c) successfully demonstrating what has been learned on course exams and course papers. The points below are basically supported by the previously reviewed research studies and provide good direction for developing an effective personal study plan.

Eighteen Summary Points

1. The amount of time devoted to relevant academic studying is highly related to the amount of learning that occurs. Thus you are advised to plan adequate amounts of study time.
2. You can modify your own study behavior by establishing personal contingency contracts in which you reward yourself for less preferred behavior (such as studying) with more preferred behavior (such as time off for a hot fudge sundae).
3. It is better for you to sleep *after* study, not *before.*

4. In order for learning to occur, you must become actively involved in the kinds of study activities that lead to the learning goal. Effective study techniques require you to *pay attention* to the material that you are responsible for learning, to *encode* it in a personally meaningful way (for example, by translating the material into your own words or perhaps by developing a mental image of it), and, finally, to *associatively link* the new material to what you already know.

5. Effective reading requires applying the three-step plan. Begin by examining the entire passage so you can decide what is important to pay attention to and learn. Next, determine the organization of each paragraph, looking for the main idea and supporting materials, and then make up questions about the passage content that you will answer in your own words. Finally, relate the new material to what you already know.

6. There is more research support for underlining and note taking than for any other study activities. Both study techniques require that you be more active than just by reading only, and also provide you with the opportunity to determine the organization of the learning material. However, only note taking really requires you to encode the material in a personally meaningful way by putting the information into your own words and then relating it to what you already know. It is clear that note taking is most likely to meet the demands that are essential for verbal learning. The research supports this by indicating a tendency for note taking to be more effective than underlining, reading only, or any other study technique.

7. If you wish to remember a point, you are much more likely to do so if you record the point in your notes. You should try to make sure your notes are correct the first time because people are likely to remember errors even after they are corrected. The most efficient notes for later retention contain as much information as possible from the lecture or textbook in as few words as possible. You should aim toward this goal as you take your notes. This will encourage you to record the really important information—the material of high-structural importance. There are a number of clues for identifying such material. Pay attention to introductory paragraphs, topic sentences, section headings, and concluding summaries.

8. When you are watching instructional films, it appears to be best for you to concentrate your attention on the film while it is being shown, to try to keep up with it, and to avoid any activities that might distract you from giving maximum attention to the fast-moving film. However, devices such as film guides can be helpful if they are distributed and completed *before* or *after* the film.

9. You can effectively build your working vocabulary by paying close attention to words you do not know, by devising a personally meaningful definition of a new word in your own words, and then by relating the new word to what you already know. Making "Vocabulary Cards" (list the new word on one side and its definition in your own words on the other side), and then using them as flash cards can be very helpful in building a bigger vocabulary.

10. Mnemonic devices (techniques to help you remember) can be very effective in organizing materials in a personally meaningful and concrete way, and in devising distinctive mental images or cues that can later be useful to you for retrieval of the learning material.

11. Recitation of previously learned material to another person who corrects your errors and adds material that was omitted can greatly enhance your later recall of the material.

12. If you use the paragraph method when you are reading textbooks (stopping after reading each paragraph to write a brief summary of what you read in as few words as possible and in your own words), it can result in increased understanding and retention.

13. Using key point cards (writing a point of particular importance on one side of a card and its definition in your own words on the other side of the card) can also be an effective study technique.

14. Reviewing previously learned material leads to increased learning and decreased amounts of forgetting. It is better for you to space reviews over a period of time than to mass or cram reviews into a short period of time because this greatly decreases long-term retention.

15. An effective method for increasing exam scores involves going through the exam four times: first, to answer all questions that are readily apparent; second, to answer questions you now remember; third, to complete the test by answering the previously unanswered questions with the answer that you first considered correct or with the second alternative if you have not already eliminated it; and, fourth, double checking the accuracy of your answers.

16. Coaching, not cramming, for standardized tests may be effective for any student who wishes to improve his or her test score. Coaching can be particularly effective for certain kinds of students such as underachievers or people who have been out of school for a period of time.

17. The nine essential steps involved in writing a good course paper include choosing a topic, writing a proposal, researching the information, analyzing the findings, writing a first draft, editing the first draft, proofreading the paper, using another person to help edit the paper, and writing a final draft. In addition, it is a good idea to read the paper out loud to yourself as a final check before submitting your work.

18. In order to provide a good answer to an essay question, it is important to know the subject matter thoroughly, to read the question carefully, and to organize your answer *before* you begin to write. A well-organized essay answer begins with an opening topic section, then presents supporting material, and ends with a concluding section.

"What to Do" Summary Checklist for Your Personal Study Plan

Read through each of the points on the checklist below and indicate your response with a check mark or by filling in the appropriate blank. Your continued use of the checklist will help you monitor your progress in actually implementing the effective study techniques that are recommended in this book.

"What to Do" Checklist

I. Developing a Personal Plan for Efficient Study
   A. Making the Most of My Study Time
      _____ 1. Because of the importance of the amount of time spent studying, I monitor my total amount of study time and the time I spend on my individual classes using the kind of Time Chart presented in Chapter 1. Total amount of study time this week (specify) _____ . Amount of study time this week for my most difficult class (specify) _____ .
      _____ 2. When I find myself needing to increase my total amount of study time or the time spent studying for a specific class, I prepare the kind of Contingency Contract shown in Chapter 1. I have found that my most effective reward for fulfilling the terms of a contract is (specify your reward) _____ .
      _____ 3. I know that the best environment for study should be well lighted, quiet, and isolated from distractions. The best place for me to study that fits these criteria is (describe) _____
      _____ .
      _____ 4. I am aware that it is better to sleep *after* I study rather than just *before* I study, and I consistently try to arrange my schedule in this way.
   B. Using This *Study Techniques* Book Most Effectively
      _____ 1. I periodically review the 18 summary points presented in Chapter 8 of *Study Techniques* in order to be sure that I remember them and continue to use them.
      _____ 2. I periodically complete this "What to Do" Checklist so that I can monitor my progress in developing a personal study plan based on these recommended study techniques.

II. Selecting Effective Study Techniques for Books, Lectures, and Films
   A. Using the Three Steps for Effective Learning
      _____ 1. I am aware of and make a continual effort to utilize the three steps to verbal learning: Pay Attention, Encode, Associate. The most recent time I particularly made a point to use this method was (describe) _____ .
      _____ 2. I specifically apply this plan to effective reading by examining the entire passage to determine what is important to pay attention to and learn, by looking at how the paragraph is organized in terms of the main idea and supporting material so I can ask myself questions about it, and, finally, by relating the content to what I already know. The last time I used this method was when I was reading (give title) _____ .
   B. Effective Study Techniques for Books, Lectures, and Films
      _____ 1. Since research studies indicate that note taking is generally more effective than reading only, underlining, or any other study technique, I make a conscientious effort to consistently use this technique.

_____ 2. I work on making my notes as correct as possible the first time since initial errors are likely to be remembered even when they are corrected later.

_____ 3. I try to make notes that include the most important main ideas from the lecture or textbook since I am most likely to remember the material that I actually record in my notes.

_____ 4. I try to make my notes efficient by recording as much important information as possible from the lecture or textbook in as few words as possible.

_____ 5. I know how to analyze the sentences or paragraphs in a passage for the high-structural importance information (topic sentences, main ideas, conclusions) that should be included in my notes whereas I omit the low-structural importance information (specific examples, supporting materials, illustrations).

_____ 6. When I am watching an instructional film, I concentrate my attention on the film while it is being shown, try to keep up with it, and avoid any distracting activities such as note taking until the film is over.

_____ 7. I continually work on building my vocabulary by paying close attention to words I do not know, by devising a personally meaningful definition of the new word in my own words, and by relating the new word to what I already know.

_____ 8. I keep a current stack of "Vocabulary Cards" as shown in Chapter 4 to use as flash cards for quizzing myself on new words I am learning. Five of the new words I am working on now are _____ , _____ , _____ , _____ , and _____ .

C. Special Study Techniques

_____ 1. I know how to use mnemonic devices (method of place, peg or hook system, rhymes, first letters, sentences, or stories, and mental image of page) to improve my memory. My most recent use of a mnemonic device was (describe) _____
_____ .

_____ 2. I am aware that recitation of previously learned material to another person who corrects my errors and adds material that I left out can increase my learning so I try to use it frequently. The last time I used recitation was when I (describe) _____
_____ .

_____ 3. I make frequent use of the paragraph method for reading my assignments by stopping at the end of each paragraph to write a brief summary in my own words of what I have read.

_____ 4. I frequently construct the kind of Key Cards described in Chapter 5 to help me study points of particular importance in lectures or textbooks.

III. Demonstrating What I Have Learned on Course Exams and Course Papers
  A. Preparing for and Taking Exams
    _____ 1. Since I am aware that reviewing previously learned material over a period of time before an exam is more successful than last-minute cramming, I work hard at using the study techniques recommended in this book to help me keep up with my classes on a regular basis.
    _____ 2. I use the "taking notes on my notes" review method discussed in Chapter 6 to help me condense, summarize, and organize the material that will be covered on an exam.
    _____ 3. I make every attempt to find out in advance the kind of test that will be given since I know that students perform better when they know the kind of test they are preparing to take. The last test I took was (describe the type of test)

    _____ ,

    and I found out in advance what kind of test to expect by (explain)

    _____ .

    _____ 4. I am familiar with the four-step plan for taking a test discussed in Chapter 6 and I attempt to use this method as I work through my tests.
    _____ 5. When I am writing the answer to an essay question, I always aim for a well-organized answer that begins with an opening topic section, then presents supporting material, and ends with a concluding section.
  B. Writing Course Papers
    _____ 1. I know the nine essential steps to writing a good course paper and I consistently practice them.
    _____ 2. I use the Final Checklist for Evaluating Course Papers given in Figure 7.1 to help me in the final editing of my papers.
    _____ 3. As a final check on my papers, I always read them out loud to myself since my ears often catch mistakes that my eyes missed.

According to Albert Jay Nock, "The mind is like the stomach. It is not how much you put into it that counts, but how much it digests."[1] It is hoped that you will find the "digestion" of all the material that you are responsible for learning less stressful and more efficient and effective as a result of developing a personal study plan that is based on the study techniques presented in this book.

Notes

1. Albert Jay Nock quoted in "Academic Survival Kit," *Nutshell 1975–76,* p. 54.

Glossary

associative linkages
establishing relationships between the new material and what you already know. *Third step of verbal learning.*

behavior modification
the process of changing behavior by rewarding the kind of behavior you want to encourage and ignoring or disapproving the behavior you want to discourage.

chunking
organizing the new information into already familiar categories.

contingency contract
a formal statement of an agreement to change behavior by making the desired reward contingent on or dependent on the completion of the less desired action. The contract should be stated in this form: *If* I do X (a specific action), *then* I will get Y (a reward).

cramming
last-minute attempt to master *new* material immediately before an exam.

"dumping papers"
a set of separate sheets of paper for each of the main points to be included in your course paper; use to record notes and information on the appropriate paper as you do your research.

encoding
the process of putting information into your own words so that it is personally meaningful. *Second step of verbal learning.*

footnote
a formal statement that gives credit to the exact source for your use of another author's actual words or direct ideas.

high-structural importance sentences
essential to the structure and meaning of the passage. Contain general statements such as topic sentences, main ideas, or conclusions.

key point cards
involves writing a brief definition or description in your own words on a file card for the most important ideas and information in the learning material.

low-structural importance sentences
can be eliminated from the passage without losing the main ideas and meaning. Contain specific examples, supporting materials, and illustrations of the higher-structural importance material.

main idea
the general topic of a paragraph or passage.

massed review
going over familiar material several times in close succession immediately before an exam.

method of place
associating a list of items to be remembered with an orderly arrangement of previously memorized physical locations.

mnemonics
methods, devices, or "tricks" for improving memory, which involve the use of mental images and mental reorganization to provide distinctive signals for later recall.

note-taking efficiency
notes that contain the most amount of information recorded in the least possible number of words.

paragraph method
involves writing a brief summary of each paragraph in the learning material using your own words and as few words as possible.

paying attention
noticing the material that you are responsible for learning. *First step of verbal learning.*

peg or hook system
a list of items to be learned are associated or "hooked" onto the "pegs" of a previously memorized rhyme containing concrete and vivid peg words. A commonly used rhyme of peg words begins "One is a bun, two is a shoe, ..."

plagiarism
involves the stealing or use of other authors' direct words or their ideas or substance without crediting the source.

Premack Principle
preferred activities can be used to reward less preferred activities.

principle of least effort
paying only surface attention to the learning material.

proofreading
rereading what you have already written to check for possible errors such as in spelling, punctuation, meaning, structure, or typographical errors.

proposal
a brief description of the course paper that you are planning to write which should include a tentative introduction and a list of sources. It is a good idea to submit this proposal to your instructor for approval before you actually begin to write.

recitation
a study method using oral summaries in order to improve your recall, understanding, and organization of the learning material.

reinforcement
supplying a reward for desired behavior and thus increasing the probability that the desired behavior will occur again.

reviewing
any effort to "go over," brush up on, or organize *previously learned* material.

spaced review
going over previously learned material over a period of time.

stimulus
a signal for a specific kind of behavior.

stimulus control of study behavior
a specific study location becomes the stimulus or signal for appropriate study behavior.

structural importance
a measure of how important a sentence is to the meaning of a paragraph or article.

successive approximations
the principle of gradually increasing the amount or quality of performance that is needed to receive the desired reward.

supporting materials
a series of sentences containing examples, explanations, clarifications, and various kinds of support for the main idea of the paragraph.

surveying
looking over the complete reading material in order to get a general idea of the important information on which you need to concentrate.

test-wiseness
knowing how to prepare for and take an exam in ways that improve test performance and reduce test anxiety.

thesis
the main idea of the paragraph, sentence, or sentences; what the author is arguing.

topic sentence

tells you the main idea of a paragraph in one sentence, which is frequently the first sentence in the paragraph.

verbal learning

information to be gained from the spoken or written word.

Index